Praise for *Unleashing Innovation*

By analyzing the business models of eleven companies in China, *Unleashing Innovation: Ten Cases from China on Digital Strategy and Market Expansion* is an insightful read for those who are seeking out new growth opportunities in today's digital and interconnected world.

Innovation, digitalization, and globalization—these three keywords are critically important for any CEO seeking to attain sustainable growth. *Unleashing Innovation* offers business leaders with the best practices and proven track record of eleven companies in China, which may be inspiring and valuable for them as they take their business to the next level.

— Soumitra Dutta, Peter Moores Dean and Professor of Management of Saïd Business School and Fellow of Balliol College, University of Oxford

How to unleash innovation in an ultra-fast changing environment? CKGSB presents 10 disruptive cases from China for inspiration.

— Léon Laulusa, Professor in the Financial Reporting and Audit department, Directeur General, Executive President and Dean, ESCP Business School

As the global economy undergoes profound changes, *Unleashing Innovation* illuminates and inspires the restructuring of the global industrial chain. I believe that once China's manufacturing industry is transformed and upgraded, it will no doubt contribute to the construction of a global ecosystem that champions win-win cooperation worldwide, and China's economic potential and corporate innovations will inject new blood to the global economy.

— Li Dongsheng, Founder and Chairman of TCL; CKGSB CEO Program Alumnus

At a time when innovation is driving the development of new FMCG brands, OATLY is at the forefront of establishing a new plant-based category and is committed to its continued development as a track that truly benefits people and the planet. This book focuses on the innovation practices of Chinese companies in the global marketplace, showing vividly how they have responded to challenges, developed new products, created new supply chains, and paved the way for China's innovation. I believe that this book provides a window for people from all walks of life to observe the Chinese innovation, and it should not be missed.

— David Zhang, President of Greater China, OATLY; CKGSB EMBA Alumnus

In a world where the global business environment evolves at breakneck speed, *Unleashing Innovation: Ten Cases from China on Digital Strategy and Market Expansion* offers an essential lens on the symbiotic dynamic between East and West. CKGSB's pivotal role in bridging these diverse markets creates a blueprint for future innovation and cross-cultural economic synergy. This book is not only timely but crucial in an era where understanding and leveraging global interconnectivity can make or break market leaders.

— Michael Hart, President, American Chamber of Commerce in China

Unleashing Innovation: Ten Cases from China on Digital Strategy and Market Expansion is a crucial guide for businesses, shedding light on the intricate interplay between Chinese and foreign enterprises. This book is an invaluable resource that not only uncovers the intricacies of China's business innovation but also provides foreign companies with valuable insights for navigating the complexities of this dynamic market. Essential reading for a comprehensive understanding of the diverse opportunities and challenges present in China's evolving business landscape.

— Rachel Tsang, Managing Director, British Chamber of Commerce in China

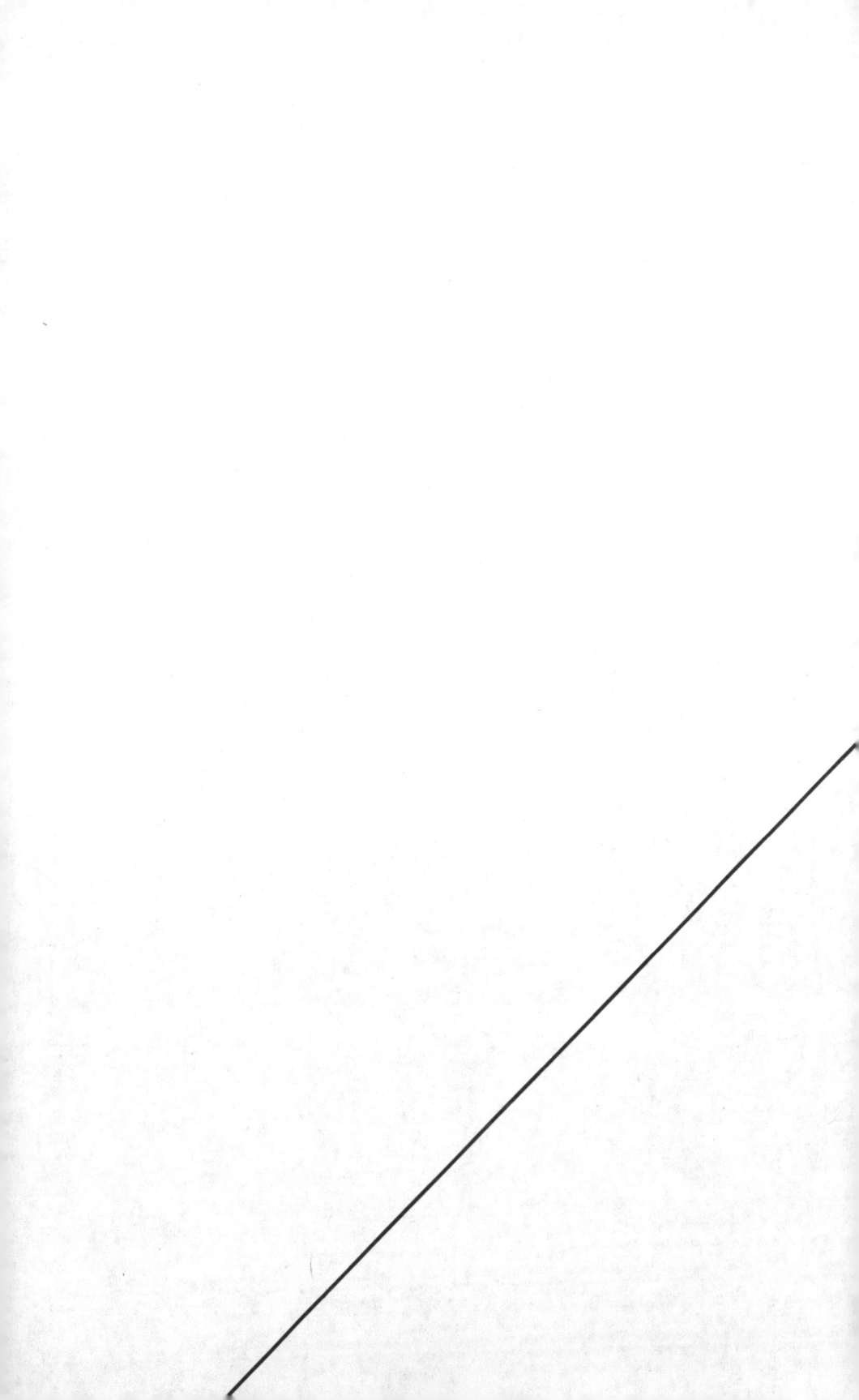

UNLEASHING INNOVATION

Ten Cases from China
on Digital Strategy and
Market Expansion

Unleashing Innovation

By Cheung Kong Graduate School of Business

ISBN-13: 978-988-8843-36-7

© 2023 Cheung Kong Graduate School of Business

BUSINESS & ECONOMICS

EB201

All rights reserved. No part of this book may be reproduced in material form, by any means, whether graphic, electronic, mechanical or other, including photocopying or information storage, in whole or in part. May not be used to prepare other publications without written permission from the publisher except in the case of brief quotations embodied in critical articles or reviews.

Published in Hong Kong by Earnshaw Books Ltd.

Contents

Foreword The Importance of Business Cases from China ⋯⋯⋯⋯⋯⋯ 4

Foreword Globalization in a Digitalized World ⋯⋯⋯⋯⋯⋯ 8

Acknowledgements ⋯⋯⋯⋯⋯⋯⋯⋯⋯⋯⋯⋯⋯⋯⋯⋯⋯⋯⋯⋯⋯⋯ 12

Chapter One: China's Digital Transformation

1 **Alibaba vs. JD.com** Business Expansion and the Flywheel Effect ⋯ 17

2 **ByteDance's Path to Globalization**
  Navigating Digital Innovation and Global Politics ⋯⋯⋯⋯⋯⋯⋯⋯ 33

3 **Banking on Data** MYbank's Innovation in Supply Chain Finance ⋯⋯ 53

Chapter Two: Changing Industrial Supply Chains

4 **Steering Toward Success?** NIO's First 10 Years as an EV Upstart ⋯ 67

5 **Rolling Forward** The Evolution of Linglong Tire ⋯⋯⋯⋯⋯⋯⋯⋯ 79

6 **Powering Ahead** How TCL Transformed and Upgraded ⋯⋯⋯⋯⋯⋯ 97

Chapter Three: Chinese Brands Meeting the Needs of Global Tastes

7 **Need for Speed**
  How SHEIN Became a Global Online Fashion Retailer ⋯⋯⋯⋯⋯⋯ 115

8 **The Cream of the Crop**
  Yili's Ambitions to Build a Global Dairy Company ⋯⋯⋯⋯⋯⋯⋯⋯ 135

Chapter Four: Western Brands Finding Success in China

9 **Milking It for All It's Worth** Oatly's China Market Entry Strategy ⋯ 151

10 **Fast Food, Fast Success** KFC's Digitalization Strategy in China ⋯⋯ 163

Faculty Biographies ⋯⋯⋯⋯⋯⋯⋯⋯⋯⋯⋯⋯⋯⋯⋯⋯⋯⋯⋯⋯ 176

About CKGSB Case Center ⋯⋯⋯⋯⋯⋯⋯⋯⋯⋯⋯⋯⋯⋯⋯⋯⋯ 186

About Cheung Kong Graduate School of Business ⋯⋯⋯⋯⋯⋯⋯⋯ 188

Foreword

The Importance of Business Cases from China

Li Wei

Professor of Economics, Associate Dean
for Asia and Director of the Case Center,
Cheung Kong Graduate School of Business

The case method is widely used in graduate business education around the world. It offers students rich contextual environments and situations, often based on real-world events, to interactively explore and discuss concepts and frameworks and to simulate the processes used to make and evaluate decisions. A well-written case can facilitate classroom discussions, reveal valuable insights on companies and markets and enhance students' skills in critical thinking, problem solving and decision making. However, when I first returned to China to teach at Cheung Kong Graduate School of Business (CKGSB) following my tenure at the Darden Graduate School of Business Administration at the University of Virginia, there was a dearth of cases applicable to local business situations. Case materials were largely based on businesses in the West, and students found it hard to apply these cases to their experiences in China.

CKGSB established the Case Center in 2003, and as China's leading business school it has since been at the forefront of producing case materials that showcase the competitive advantages of a wide range of businesses in China and, more broadly, Asia. With our world-class faculty and research, combined with our unparalleled alumni network in the Greater China region and beyond, CKGSB aspires to advance business education through the development of high-quality Asia-focused business cases. Our portfolio of more than 500 cases comprises one of the school's many invaluable knowledge assets, spanning industries, geographical regions and business disciplines. We are proud that each case is based on a deep understanding of the Chinese and Asian markets and is developed in line with rigorous research standards. CKGSB's cases have not only served as teaching materials in the classroom but also as valuable sources of business insights for a wider audience, ranging from executives working in global companies to media outlets such as *The Financial Times*, *Harvard Business Review* and *Caixin*.

China has experienced remarkable economic growth over the past few decades, transforming itself into a global economic superpower. Chinese businesses have become hotbeds of innovation and technological advancement, and the country has produced numerous successful companies that have achieved remarkable growth and global influence. These transformations continue to have major implications for international business and for the global business community and the need for more in-depth understanding of China's historical and future economic Transformation has never been greater. Having an ever-larger portfolio of cases on businesses in China can help bridge the knowledge gap and provide practical insights for business executives and researchers to navigate the intricacies of the China market, and further contribute to the global understanding of China's economic development.

Unleashing Innovation: Ten Cases from China on Digital Strategy and Market Expansion serves as a testament to the commitment of CKGSB and its community of dedicated researchers, alumni, and esteemed faculty in this regard. We wanted to highlight eleven companies, which in recent years have been riding the waves of the digital revolution and globalization as they digitalize and tap into unchartered markets, using innovative strategies and technological upgrades to transform their businesses.

The book is conceptually organized into four parts. It first examines how China's homegrown technology companies transformed themselves to meet the changing global environment. It then focuses on Chinese companies that revolutionized the industrial supply chain. The third section highlights the growth strategies of Chinese brands going global to meet the needs of consumers worldwide. The final section looks at the development and success of foreign companies operating in China which have innovated through digitalization and new strategies. Through these cases, we explore the approaches these companies adopted to unleash innovation, develop cutting-edge digital technologies and compete globally.

On the list of the 2023 Fortune Global 500, 142 of the companies are headquartered in Greater China, more than any other country. Together their revenues in 2022 accounted for $11.7 trillion, 29% of the total revenue of all companies on the list. According to CB Insights, by mid-year

2023 Greater China had 180 unicorn companies, representing around 15% of the global total.

Since 2015, CKGSB has been committed to building a global ecosystem that fosters a new generation of economic disruptors with an enhanced emphasis on global responsibility, social purpose and a long-term perspective. To date, more than 1,000 founders of companies with at least Series A funding have studied at CKGSB, including the founders of 136 unicorn companies in total and 38 unicorn companies listed on CB Insights (2017-2022).

The stories of businesses pursuing digital ambitions or navigating hyper-competitive markets are always fascinating to me and my CKGSB colleagues, and we are extremely privileged to be able to learn about these stories first-hand from those who played an important role in these companies. We found that many of the stories warranted careful examination and analysis by our students, and in turn, we hope this book of selected cases offers readers a deeper understanding of the factors and individuals behind the unique journeys of these businesses.

Foreword

Globalization in a Digitalized World

Zhou Li

Assistant Dean,
Cheung Kong Graduate School of Business

The way globalization is viewed is changing, both in the face of recent formidable challenges but also with the rapid increase in digitalization that is taking place all over the world. What's more, geopolitical issues abound and consequently the business environment for companies working internationally is getting more difficult to navigate, but it remains true that only those who continue to globalize will win out in the long run.

Thanks to the now inter- and intra-national nature of the global supply chain, we find ourselves in an irreversibly global market, reliant upon physical resources, knowledge and expertise from around the world. Thus, for businesses, future success lies in maintaining access to resources, and for business people, success requires the commitment to learning from the experiences of peers around the world.

The Cheung Kong Graduate School of Business (CKGSB) has always been committed to its role as a global learning platform, collating and analyzing worldwide business insights and sharing them to help businesses and their people grow. *Unleashing Innovation: Ten Cases from China on Digital Strategy and Market Expansion* provides the opportunity to share the knowledge we have accrued, hopefully providing a resource that helps explain the successes of and challenges faced by, global businesses.

The book first looks at some of the Chinese companies playing a world-leading role in the digital transformation of business. Platform companies such as Alibaba and JD.com were born of digitalization and have revolutionized business practices in so many ways. Through digitalization, companies such as TCL and Linglong Tire have transformed their manufacturing and supply chain management processes, allowing them to continue their global expansion and to challenge market leaders. The book also include examples of new businesses that have, right from the start, adopted unique digital strategies. EV manufacturer NIO, for example, sells its cars as part of a "lifestyle" rather than simply a mode of transportation and MYbank has revolutionized access to financing for micro-, small- and medium-sized enterprises.

The cases also include examples of Chinese companies that have managed to succeed globally despite the current economic headwinds, showing that it is possible for any business, in almost any sector, to go global if they adopt the right approach. As a platform company, ByteDance has experienced immense success with Douyin in China and with its sister app TikTok in the rest of the world, despite facing many regulatory challenges. Dairy company Yili has taken a more traditional approach to global expansion. Even though it started in a country that has a high-level of lactose-intolerant consumers, it has gone on to become a mainstay in markets around the world. Online fashion retailer SHEIN has also shown that while a home market is important, there can be benefits to choosing another country as your main target market.

Of course, the China market is also a lucrative target, given its size. And while it is a notoriously difficult arena in which to succeed, there are examples of both long-established and newly-arriving companies achieving success. If they can do it, then so can anyone with the right approach. KFC has had its ups and downs in China, but it is now well-established as one of the country's most popular fast-food brands. And new arrival Oatly demonstrates how an innovative marketing strategy driven by strong local leadership can carve out a market for entirely new products.

The world we live in today, despite its difficulties, is still a connected one, with shared digital networks, shared problems and shared solutions. We are faced by numerous global issues, such as climate change, which require the sharing of knowledge and expertise from a wide range of international parties in order for a solution to be found. The best way to succeed is through learning from each other and working together.

We hope that *Unleashing Innovation: Ten Cases from China on Digital Strategy and Market Expansion* can go some way to help the process of global learning and help readers build knowledge, solve problems and better execute successful business strategies that help improve the global quality of life.

Acknowledgements

This book is the outcome of the rigorous research and original thinking of the CKGSB professors and researchers mentioned hereafter, who are all dedicated to developing new management theories stemming from Asia for the global business community. We are grateful for their unique perspectives, analytical thinking and quest to pursue the truth in business. In particular, we would like to thank Li Wei, Associate Dean and Professor of Economics at CKGSB, for his work in directing the Case Center and for his support for this book.

We are grateful to our colleagues at the CKGSB Case Center — in particular, Chen Jian, Meng Fanyi and Qiao Yiyuan — and the Global Marketing and Communications team — Ira Zaka, Tian Xuefang, Joseph Duckworth, Jessica Wang, Liu Xuan and Dong Kunyu — for their expertise, dedication and efforts in writing, editing, producing and launching this book.

Last but not least, we thank Juliet London, who edited the book for the better; Heather Mowbray, who contributed to translation; Midori Katakura at Flow Asia, whose creative designs added vibrancy to the cases; and Graham Earnshaw and Patrick Body at Earnshaw Books for proofreading and publishing this book.

Chapter One

China's Digital Transformation

The story of how China's digital giants have developed provides insights into the interplay of data, digital strategy and global market navigation. From MYbank's strategic utilization of data in the reshaping of supply chain finance to the intriguing competitive and cooperative dynamics between Alibaba and JD.com, and ByteDance's strategic global expansion in the face of regulatory challenges, these case studies provide an understanding of the ways in which digitalization has been integrated into the business models of China's digital giants, thereby accelerating growth.

Case Studies

1 Alibaba vs. JD.com
Business Expansion and the Flywheel Effect

2 ByteDance's Path to Globalization
Navigating Digital Innovation and Global Politics

3 Banking on Data
MYbank's Innovation in Supply Chain Finance

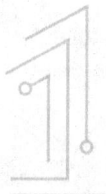

Alibaba vs JD.com
Business Expansion and the Flywheel Effect

Li Wei, Professor of Economics, Associate Dean for Asia and Director of the Case Center, Cheung Kong Graduate School of Business

Chen Jian, Assistant Director, Case Center, Cheung Kong Graduate School of Business

In 2021, on Singles' Day, China's largest annual online shopping festival, Alibaba's Tmall recorded a gross merchandise volume (GMV) of RMB 540 billion (USD 84 billion), an 8.5% year-on-year (YoY) increase. Meanwhile, JD.com achieved a GMV of RMB 349 billion (USD 54 billion), a 28.6% YoY increase. While these rates of growth were lower than in previous years, they were still impressive given the level of competition between these two well-established e-commerce players.

Having profited greatly from the explosion of online business in China over the last two decades, Alibaba and JD.com have continued to diversify their e-commerce-dependent growth models and to branch out into other business sectors. At the end of 2019, Daniel Zhang, the then CEO of Alibaba, proposed three new strategic pillars for this Chinese tech behemoth, which he reaffirmed in 2023: globalization, domestic consumption and big data powered by cloud computing. Meanwhile, in 2021, then President of JD.com Xu Lei said the company's focus would be on digital upgrading and the decentralization of its retail business.

While JD.com's revenue in 2021 exceeded that of Alibaba by more than RMB 100 billion (USD 15.5 billion), Alibaba had more than ten times the net profit of JD.com and twice as many active users.

This case study will examine how Alibaba and JD.com have each carved out their success over the last two decades, based on two very different models of e-commerce.

The flywheel effect

The "flywheel effect," first coined by Jim Collins in his 2001 book *Good to Great,* provides a useful reference to understand the business models of Alibaba and JD.com. The flywheel effect describes the process whereby small victories accumulated over time will eventually gain sufficient momentum to become self-sustaining, similar to the process of a mechanical flywheel. While it may initially require a lot of effort to turn a flywheel from a static position, once it begins to rotate, the entire gear set will follow and soon the flywheel will spin easily.

Alibaba's flywheel model

The rise of Taobao

Alibaba entered the B2B market in 2002, but soon faced a significant challenge when, in 2003, eBay purchased the Chinese e-commerce firm Eachnet.com as a means to break into the Chinese market. Concerned that Eachnet.com could take market share from 1688.com, Alibaba's wholesale platform, in 2003, Alibaba founder Jack Ma gathered together a small team to launch Taobao (淘宝), which translates as "hunting for treasure." According to Ma, "eBay wanted to buy the entire Chinese market while we wanted to create an online marketplace in China."

While Eachnet.com functioned as a conventional online customer-to-customer (C2C) bidding platform, Taobao took a revolutionary approach to the e-commerce industry, enabling individuals and small business owners to sell their products by setting up their own stores.

Taobao's success was both immediate and astounding. By 2005, annual revenue was already RMB 8 billion (USD 977 million), exceeding that of Walmart China. In terms of transaction volume and the number of products available on its platform, in 2005 Taobao surpassed Yahoo! Japan to become Asia's largest online marketplace. Within four years of being founded, Taobao had amassed 30 million registered users and was offering goods spanning digital products, apparel, cosmetics, virtual goods and jewelry. Taobao utilized a long-tail strategy, creating a huge online marketplace of specialized and difficult-to-find products.

In 2003, Alipay was launched, providing a quicker, more secure way to send and receive money on Taobao. Prior to Alipay, a lack of confidence between buyers and sellers had frequently resulted in failed transactions, with customers uncertain as to whether they would receive items they had ordered. To solve this problem, Alipay held the funds in escrow until the buyer had received their purchase. In 2004, a year after Taobao's release, with his focus on constantly improving the platform, Jack Ma introduced Aliwangwang, a messaging platform that allowed buyers and sellers to communicate with one another via text, voice and video messaging.

To get the flywheel spinning, Alibaba constructed a network of merchants and consumers without actually directly dealing with or owning the rights to any of the products on its platform. Instead, it has operated as an "information intermediary," building efficient platforms for information exchange. And as its user base expands, Alibaba has been able to lower its transactions fees, increasing its competitiveness.

Boosting traffic through Tmall and other new businesses

While Taobao played a crucial role in laying the foundation for traffic on Alibaba's platform and in building momentum for the flywheel effect, Ma had always envisioned Alibaba as a "pan-e-commerce business" that could serve as an information service provider for numerous industries. The next step toward achieving this ambition was the 2008 launch of Tmall, Alibaba's business-to-consumer (B2C) platform. Tmall enabled third-party brands to sell their products through franchised stores.

Sellers on Taobao often found themselves competing with merchants selling counterfeit goods. With the launch of Tmall, Alibaba raised the entry threshold, only allowing licensed brands to set up stores on the platform. It was a move that succeeded in attracting numerous renowned Chinese and international brands, many of them having previously been reluctant to sign up.

Tmall also helped diversify Alibaba's revenue streams beyond transaction fees and advertising, allowing the company to generate revenue from establishment fees, sales commissions, warehousing, delivery and online marketing services.

Alibaba's rapid expansion was based upon the ecosystem of consumers and businesses across its various platforms. Earlier, in 2007, Alibaba had introduced Alimama, a digital marketing and advertising service platform that served Taobao and subsequently Tmall. Within four years of its establishment, Alimama had eclipsed Baidu as the most popular advertising platform in China. In 2010, Alibaba launched AliExpress, an international e-commerce platform that enabled small and medium-sized businesses in China and other locations to sell to consumers overseas. Sellers on AliExpress often lack access to local markets as well as the expertise on how to promote their products, marketing-savvy individuals and small businesses recognize the opportunity to purchase goods from them at wholesale prices on AliExpress and resell these goods to customers worldwide. Additionally, in the same year, Alibaba established Juhuasuan, a group-buying and marketing platform, to supplement the business ecosystem.

On the basis of the success of Alipay, which had been used as a payment service for Taobao since 2003, Alibaba went on to expand its payment service business, establishing Ant Financial in 2013. Later rebranded as Ant Group, this entity offered easier and cheaper access to financial services for consumers and small businesses, integrating them into a financial ecosystem covering credit, insurance and wealth management services.

Alibaba's supply chain transformation: Cainiao network

Even though Alibaba had established a comprehensive ecosystem of businesses, in 2013 it was still lacking a sophisticated supply chain infrastructure, and remained heavily reliant upon third-party logistics providers to deliver its goods. Taobao was also struggling to keep up with the huge demand of managing product returns.

This led Alibaba to team up with eight logistics companies in China in 2013, jointly launching Cainiao Network, its logistics arm. The platform has evolved to serve Taobao and Tmall as well as other merchants and companies. In 2021, Cainiao delivered on average over 4 million packages per day.

More recently, Alibaba has extended its ecosystem into lifestyle services. In 2016, it launched its online-to-offline (O2O) supermarket chain, Hema, which guarantees to deliver groceries purchased at one of its stores within 30 minutes. In 2018, Alibaba purchased the catering and food delivery company Ele.me, merging it with its own brand Koubei to expand into sectors including travel, beauty, food delivery, and entertainments.

While Alibaba started as a platform to connect buyers and sellers, its business expansion strategy over the last two decades has become increasingly sophisticated. Its functions now extend into areas such as advertising, marketing, finance and logistics. It is noteworthy that whichever business Alibaba is in, the rationale for its growth is to attract traffic to its information intermediary.

Alibaba's main revenue streams are commercial transactions, cloud computing, media and entertainment and digital business. In 2021, commercial transactions — which include Alibaba's retail, international and wholesale businesses and the Cainiao logistics service — accounted for 87% of the company's total revenue. Domestic retail accounted for 66% of the revenue from commercial transactions. Contrary to a popular perception that Alibaba's main revenue generator is from transactional commissions, within its retail business, 30% of revenue comes from advertising, while only 12% stems from commissions on transactions.

Figure 1   Alibaba's revenue structure, 2021

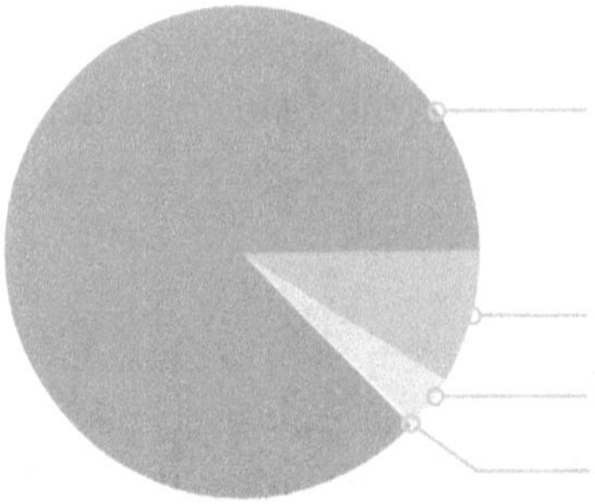

Commercial transactions	87.1%
Cloud computing	8.7%
Media and entertainment	3.9%
Digital business	0.4%

Source: Alibaba annual report

Empowering others with information and data

In 2016, Jack Ma introduced the groundbreaking concept of "new retail," a vision that challenged the dominance of pure e-commerce and foreshadowed the imminent transformation of the retail industry. This concept sparked widespread discussion among media, business professionals and academia, highlighting the need to adapt to an evolving market landscape. Interestingly, within a year, JD.com, also began embracing the idea of "borderless retail." Xu Lei, JD.com's Chief Marketing Officer at that time, acknowledged the profound changes affecting all stakeholders, including consumers, supply chains and marketing strategies.

Online retail is no longer producing the massive dividends that it once did. In this new stage of development, as e-commerce experiences slowing growth rates and increasing saturation, Alibaba has shifted its strategy away from relying solely on platform traffic toward providing information services to other companies.

More recently, Alibaba has been collaborating with a range of organizations, particularly brick-and-mortar retailers such as Bailian Group, to whom it provides traffic and data services to help them integrate their offline stores, merchandise, logistics and payment tools.

Figure 2   Alibaba's growth flywheel

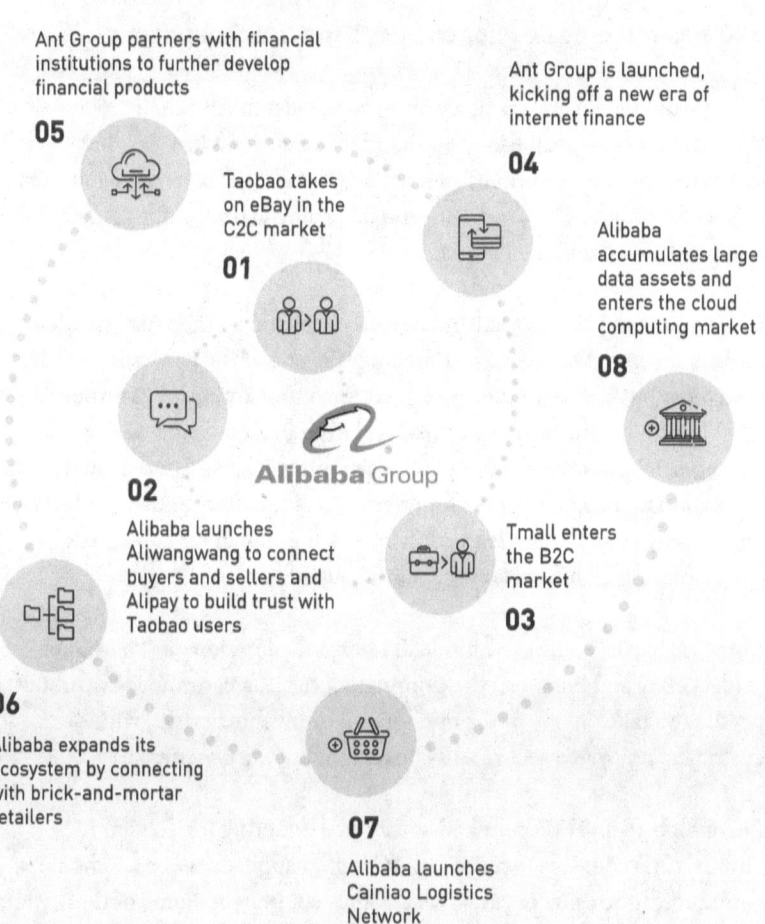

Source: CKGSB Case Center

JD.com's flywheel model

B2C e-commerce developed due to the SARS pandemic

JD.com emerged from the brick-and-mortar electronics chain 360buy. With its first store established by founder Richard Liu in 1998, 360buy soon expanded to set up multiple branches around China. Later, JD Multimedia was set up to distribute magneto-optical products from Zhongguancun, Beijing's key technology district.

In 2002, just as Liu was ready to expand his business, the SARS pandemic broke out across Greater China. Beijing was one of the hardest hit areas, with most businesses in the city forced to halt operations. Liu responded quickly, moving his business online and even personally delivering packages. With the re-opening of the economy, JD.com soon gained a reputation among consumers for offering high quality goods with low prices and fast delivery. Liu made the decision to shut down his company's offline stores, placing all his bets on the online business.

In the early 2000s, the C2C model had exploded in popularity. Market leaders eBay and Eachnet.com dominated, earning commissions without needing to take on any of the operational or inventory risks, while customers enjoyed a secure and convenient buying experience.

Liu and his team at JD.com had considered adopting the C2C model. However, JD.com was focused on "3C digital appliances," i.e., computers, communication and consumer electronics equipment. Some of these were high-end, requiring a level of quality control and after-sales services that could not be guaranteed through a C2C approach. Consequently, Liu chose to launch his JD.com platform in the business-to-consumer (B2C) sector. He adopted a direct sales model, sourcing products from authorized suppliers before selling them directly to consumers.

In contrast to the "information intermediary" model adopted by Alibaba, the JD.com model was based on the idea of a "merchant intermediary," profiting from the price differential between buying and selling products. With this approach, JD.com bears liability for inventory risks and expenses, while placing a greater emphasis on metrics, such as gross profit margins, asset turnover and product quality.

Figure 3 Comparison of Taobao and JD.com's e-commerce models

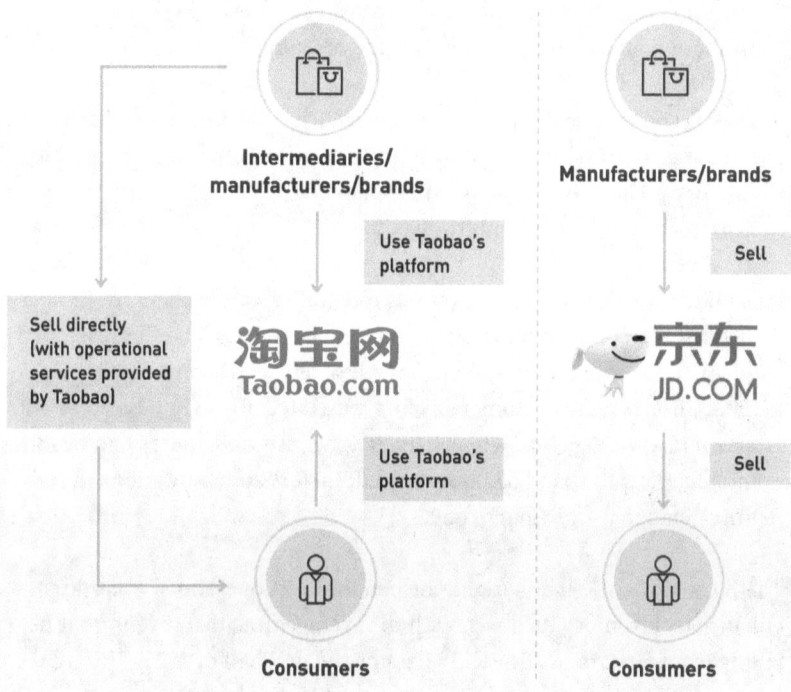

Source: CKGSB Case Center

JD.com's self-built logistics network

With the e-commerce industry in China maturing, JD.com recognized the need to expand its offerings and revenue streams. In 2010, the company launched its third-party vendor platform, known as POP (platform open plan), through which external merchants were able to sell their products. POP greatly increased the quantity and variety of products available to customers and enabled JD.com to expand its revenue streams, with income now also coming from platform licensing, commissions, warehouse and distribution fees and marketing.

Brands were drawn to the POP platform due to the flexibility it offered: they could choose to either have JD.com manage their online store on their behalf or manage the store independently utilizing the JD.com distribution network. JD.com also worked with purchasing agents overseas to meet consumers' demands for products outside of China.

Today, JD.com has developed into a comprehensive online retailer selling a wide range of physical goods including books, clothing, daily necessities and luxury goods. The company has expanded further into virtual fields such as healthcare, music and travel.

JD.com owes much of its success to its integrated supply chain. In its early days, the company's infrastructure had been largely underdeveloped and logistics companies frequently failed to deliver JD.com's costly merchandise, leaving customers feeling frustrated. This led JD.com to establish its own logistics network in 2007, whose warehouses and facilities eventually grew to span 50,000 square kilometers across locations in Beijing, Shanghai and Guangzhou.

The JD.com logistics network has helped lower its operation costs and enhance its inventory turnover, with the average time that inventory is held falling from 50 days in 2011 to 28 days by the first half of 2021. Through the implementation of smart warehousing at its fulfilment centers around China — with automated drones on occasion being used for last-mile delivery — and through its cloud platform, fulfilment costs dropped from 7% in 2011 to around 6% by 2021.

Supply chain finance

Since 2013, JD Finance (later renamed JD Digits) has provided loans, payment solutions, asset management, crowdfunding and other financial services to individuals and small companies. JD Digits assists self-operating suppliers and high-quality third-party merchants with purchasing, warehousing and settlement guarantee funds. Through its supply chain finance, JD Digits has mitigated the long-existing financial risks for JD.com's brick-and-mortar suppliers by providing them with easier access to finance, which has, in turn, increased JD.com's supply chain efficiency.

In summary, the JD.com expansion strategy has centered around its vertically integrated commodity supply chain. JD.com got the flywheel spinning through a merchant intermediary model with value-added services.

JD.com's main revenue sources are two-fold. It earns most of its income from the products it sells directly on its platform: a whopping 90% of JD.com revenue comes from its self-operating business. The remainder is generated by services provided, including fees from third-party merchants using its platform, advertising and logistics services.

Figure 4   Revenue structure of JD.com

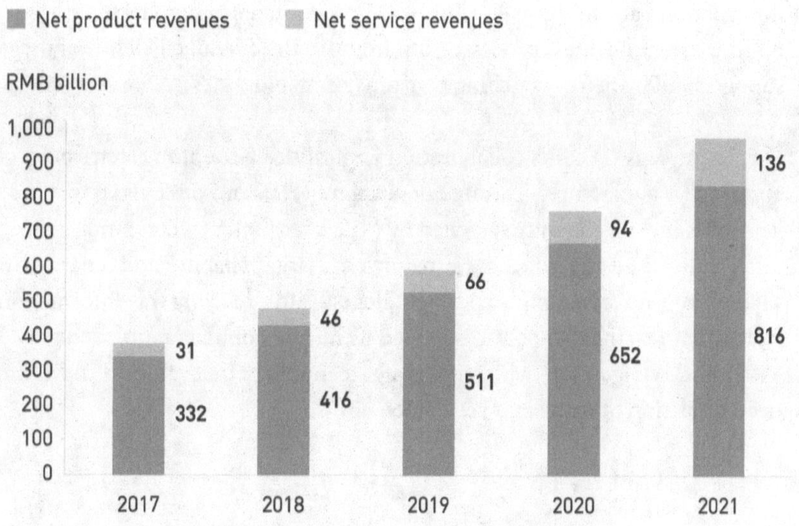

■ Net product revenues   ■ Net service revenues

RMB billion

Year	Net product revenues	Net service revenues
2017	332	31
2018	416	46
2019	511	66
2020	652	94
2021	816	136

Sources: JD.com annual reports, EO Intelligence, 36kr, CKGSB Case Center

Empowering others with supply chain services

Extending beyond e-commerce, in order to drive new growth, JD.com has shifted its focus. In an internal company letter in 2017, Liu emphasized that "the nature of retail has never changed — it has always been about costs, efficiency and user experience. But as technology develops and consumption upgrades, the value created changes. In the future, JD.com will focus on service infrastructure and will provide retail-as-a-service solutions to the whole of society."

In May 2021, JD Logistics was spun off from JD.com. In China, it has collaborated with companies such as Skechers, Unilever and other MNCs to enhance their logistics operations.

JD.com has reconstructed its supply chain ecosystem by implementing a customer-to-manufacturer (C2M) model. This model accommodates large manufacturers, brand owners, merchants, third-party logistics companies and retailers. Unlike traditional supply chain models, where suppliers and brands sell directly to consumers, JD.com relays sales and customer information back to suppliers. This C2M model enables suppliers to optimize their business processes and improve the overall efficiency of the supply chain by better matching consumer demand.

One example is JD.com's collaboration with Midea Group, an electrical appliance manufacturer. Through data analysis, JD.com discovered that the keywords most frequently searched by Midea customers when purchasing refrigerators had shifted from terms such as "large capacity" and "energy saving" to "preserving high-end ingredients." After relaying this information back to Midea, the company developed its hugely popular "multi-door Vitamin C refrigerator," which integrates technology that can slow down the decomposition of fruits and vegetables.

Figure 5   JD.com's growth flywheel

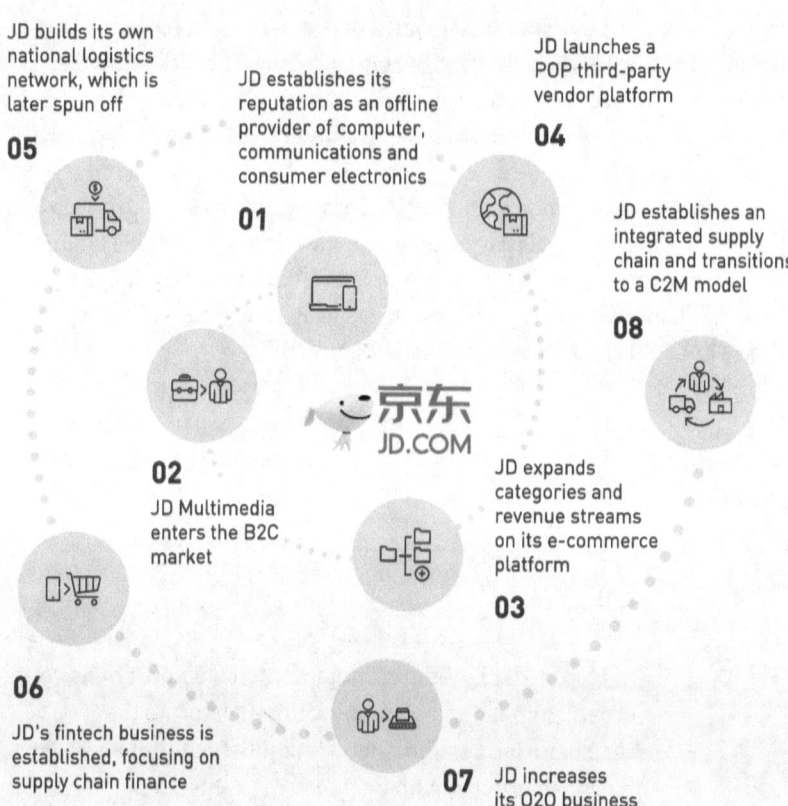

Source: CKGSB Case Center

Two flywheel models, two success stories

In conclusion, the developmental journeys of Alibaba and JD.com demonstrate the flywheel effect in operation. While Alibaba's flywheel model has primarily centered around the "information intermediary" market, JD.com has operated as a more traditional "merchant intermediary."

The fundamental differences in their e-commerce business models led to their distinctive flywheel structures, which have formed the basis for a rivalry that stretches back nearly two decades. With both businesses having recently changed their respective strategic goals, only time will tell whether they will be able to maintain their rates of growth.

Updates

Alibaba

In March 2023, Alibaba implemented a comprehensive organizational and governance restructuring. The restructuring resulted in the establishment of six major business groups, with each group granted a high level of autonomy and independence:

- Taobao and Tmall Group, which includes Taobao, Tmall, Xianyu and 1688.com
- Alibaba International Digital Commerce Group, which includes Lazada, AliExpress, Trendyol and Alibaba.com
- Local Services Group, which mainly includes the food delivery business of Ele.me and the navigation business of Amap
- Cainiao Network

- Cloud Intelligence Group, which includes Alibaba Cloud, DingTalk and other businesses
- Digital Media and Entertainment Group, which includes Youku, Damai and Alibaba Pictures.

The early signs are that the turnaround plans are bearing fruit, with all six divisions reporting solid revenue growth and improvements in profitability. Groupwide revenue for the quarter ended June 30, 2023 grew by 14% YoY, and operating income surged 70%.

JD.com

In March 2023, two subsidiaries of JD.Com, JD Industrials and JD Property, filed for IPOs in Hong Kong. It is estimated that each of the deals could be worth more than USD 1 billion.

According to the filings, JD.com has expressed its intention to retain a stake of over 50% in the units following the proposed spin-offs.

ByteDance's Path to Globalization
Navigating Digital Innovation and Global Politics

Xiang Bing, Founding Dean and Professor of China Business and Globalization, Cheung Kong Graduate School of Business

Teng Bingsheng, Professor of Strategic Management and Associate Dean for Strategic Research, Cheung Kong Graduate School of Business

Yan Min, Researcher, Case Center, Cheung Kong Graduate School of Business

Until its signature product, TikTok, was blocked in India and subjected to intense scrutiny by U.S. authorities, ByteDance had been viewed as among the most successful and globalized Chinese internet companies. Despite these setbacks, ByteDance continues to develop rapidly. According to technology magazine *The Information*, ByteDance's 2022 revenue surpassed USD 80 billion, up more than 30% on 2021. In March 2023, Shou Zi Chew, CEO of TikTok, stated that the app had 150 million monthly active users (MAU) in the U.S. alone.

ByteDance's trajectory is nothing short of remarkable, and this case study endeavors to unveil the pivotal milestones in its extraordinary journey. It delves into the strategies that enabled ByteDance to forge sensational brands like Toutiao, Douyin and TikTok. It examines whether there remains scope for ByteDance to improve its international expansion strategies and will look to the future to suggest what may lie ahead for the company.

Figure 1 ByteDance product portfolio

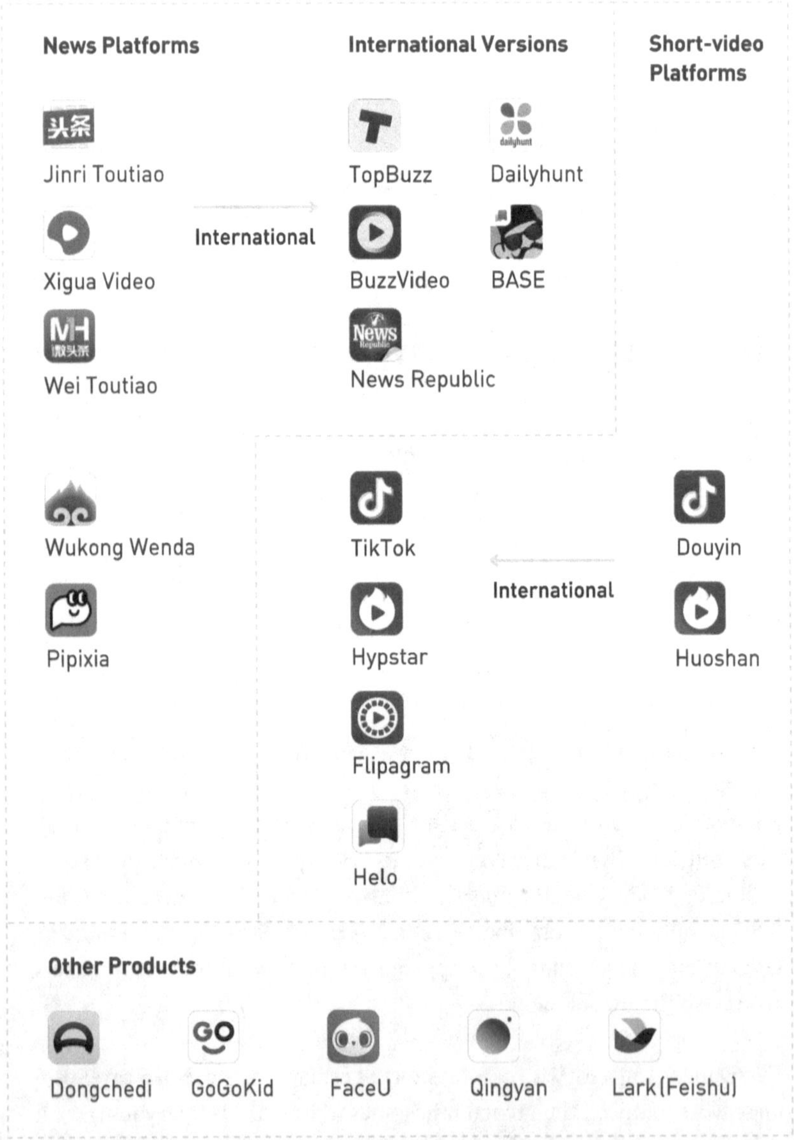

News Platforms
- Jinri Toutiao
- Xigua Video
- Wei Toutiao
- Wukong Wenda
- Pipixia

→ International →

International Versions
- TopBuzz
- BuzzVideo
- News Republic
- TikTok
- Hypstar
- Flipagram
- Helo

Short-video Platforms
- Dailyhunt
- BASE
- Douyin
- Huoshan

← International ←

Other Products
- Dongchedi
- GoGoKid
- FaceU
- Qingyan
- Lark (Feishu)

Sources: ByteDance website, Huachuang Securities

Toutiao and the debut of ByteDance

Zhang Yiming, founder of ByteDance, set off on what was to become an epic entrepreneurial journey in 2005, immediately after graduating from Nankai University with a bachelor's degree in software engineering. By the end of 2011, Zhang had already achieved significant success as founder and CEO of 99fang.com, a real estate information provider. However, he had greater ambitions to create something more significant and outstanding. Recognizing the limited potential of his then "search engine" business, Zhang identified the immense possibilities of mobile apps and the wealth of information they could offer.

The story goes that at a meeting in a café with an investor, Wang Qiong, in January 2012, Zhang sketched out a plan on a napkin. He explained how he wanted to build an app that would use big data to analyze a user's news preferences and to offer curated content. Wang recognized the potential of Zhang's proposal and agreed on the spot to invest USD 80,000. In August that year, the Toutiao app was launched.

The battle for information services on smartphones

For centuries, written media had been dominated by the printed format. But with Steve Jobs' re-invention of the mobile phone in the early 2000s, news consumption increasingly shifted to the screens of handheld devices. Newspapers, journals and press websites were soon looking antiquated and ran the risk of becoming obsolete.

It felt like a race against time, with media companies and portal sites rushing to update their apps and to stay relevant. The competition for attention for mobile information in China hit a peak in 2013, when there were more than 1,300 apps offering news-related information. However, many of these apps struggled to attract investors, since they lacked any business viability beyond channeling information acquired from other websites. They were improbable competitors against the established internet behemoths. Even in the creative and entrepreneurial environment of the U.S., it seemed unimaginable that a newcomer could take on the established providers.

Given the highly competitive context into which it was launched, Toutiao's accomplishments are all the more remarkable. In 2014, less than two years after that fateful café meeting, the company received USD 100 million in Series C funding, had 120 million registered users, 40 million of whom were MAU, and was valued at USD 500 million.

Toutiao's success can be attributed to four key factors.

First, a succinct name: In Chinese, the full app name "Jinri Toutiao" (今日头条) literally means "today's headlines." Right from the start, Toutiao told users what the app would deliver.

Second, from the outset, Toutiao offered unmatched quality. At a time when traditional news outlets were still only updating once or twice per day, Toutiao constantly provided users with new content every time they refreshed the page. This was further enhanced by Zhang's introduction of a personalized recommendation engine in 2012, utilizing AI-based technology to tailor content for each user. The code remains the foundation for the "For You" feeds on TikTok today.

Third, using a very deliberate promotional strategy, Zhang worked to ensure the product was available to the largest possible audience as a pre-installed app on mobile phones, supported by substantial marketing campaigns on Weibo, a leading Chinese microblogging website. These efforts helped drive the number of daily active users (DAU) to more than 10 million in Toutiao's first year of activity.

Lastly, there was a focus on generating profit. By delivering customized content to users, the app successfully established a strong foundation for its advertising function. This contributed to Toutiao's positive cash flow within a year of its debut, an unprecedented achievement at that time.

Operation mode: algorithm + content

For more than half a decade, Zhang's recommendation engine remained an unknown black box to outsiders. But in January 2018, after its fourth major upgrade, the algorithm used by Toutiao was revealed by Cao

Huanhuan, Principal Research Engineer, one of the company's senior algorithm architects.

In general terms, the algorithm features a quantification process to determine user satisfaction with the content served by the app, with adjustments according to other exogenous variables, such as user profiles and environmental characteristics. Using this structure, the algorithm deduces whether the recommended content is suitable for a user in a certain scenario, fulfilling its ultimate goal of matching relevant content to the needs of individual users.

There is no doubt that Toutiao's methodologies and technological strengths gave it the edge over traditional media. However, using third-party sources precipitated numerous lawsuits for copyright infringement. Toutiao's response was to work cooperatively with traditional media, and by 2019, Toutiao had established partnerships with around 10,000 media outlets.

Another fundamental element in the strength of the Toutiao product came with the September 2014 launch of "Toutiaohao." Similar to the way that WeChat's official accounts support the creation of user-generated content (UGC), Toutiaohao has helped build content on Toutiao. Account holders can publish various types of content, such as text, images, videos and polls. This content is then distributed to relevant users, alongside the Toutiao news content. Toutiao has invested heavily in its UGC, far more so than its competitors. In 2017, for example, it spent RMB 1.5 billion (USD 222 million) on UGC.

The profit model and personalized ad recommendations via news feed

In the early days of website development, user experience had often been compromised by banner ads and obtrusive flash animation sprawling across web pages. Toutiao cleverly sidestepped this problem, working to develop a synergy between advertisers and users. There are three key elements to the success of Toutiao's advertising operations.

First, there has been a focus on making advertisements informative, with a similar look and feel to content pieces. According to Toutiao, advertising is more likely to be effective if it includes relevant information, working with the type of interests and flow of information being provided to users. Second, Toutiao provides a degree of personalization, often making multiple versions of an advertisement, with a particular version pushed to individual users based on their browsing history, likes and favorites. Third, Toutiao embraced video advertising early on, incorporating this format in 2016, well ahead of many competitors.

Figure 2　Monthly active users of Toutiao and other news information apps

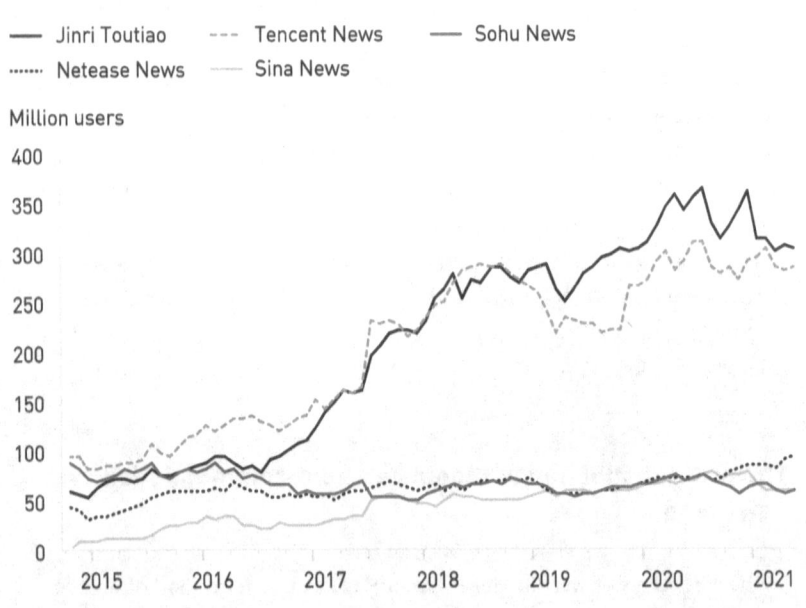

Source: Wind Information

Growth and challenges

Based on its success in the Chinese market, Toutiao embarked on a mission to conquer the global market. Its first international product, "TopBuzz," was launched in North America in August 2015 and shortly thereafter in Brazil and Japan. Using the same strategy that had worked in China, including closely cooperating with media organizations on copyright and encouraging UGC, TopBuzz attracted a solid volume of downloads. However, with insufficient investment and bottlenecks in content supply, TopBuzz struggled to replicate Toutiao's success.

The competitive landscape was also markedly different. In the U.S., scuffles between media and tech giants had already been underway for several years. Fox and CNN were committed to promoting their respective mobile apps, while Google News had integrated personalized recommendations into its mobile app as early as 2006. Meanwhile, Facebook was lacing up its gloves and already had one billion MAU. Minor local competitors, such as Flipboard, would regularly emerge. Within this environment, TopBuzz, a foreign outsider, struggled to find a foothold.

Meanwhile, back in China, Toutiao was booming. By 2015, it had 300 million registrations and 35 million DAU. Every day, users were spending more than 1.5 billion minutes on the app. That year, the number of staff at Toutiao increased from 300 to more than 1,300 and its valuation in the private equity market also rose dramatically.

In summary, from 2012 to 2015, Toutiao achieved massive success in the Chinese market. Within its first two years of operation, it had become the top news app in the country and had achieved profitability. The experience of finding success through a startup proved invaluable to Zhang, the young entrepreneur, and the team around him.

The short video boom and Douyin

Toutiao launched its short video channel in May 2015. Within 18 months, by September 2016, daily video views exceeded one billion, surpassing text and pictures to become the platform's most popular form of content. This prompted Zhang to rethink the company's strategic focus and to shift to short video as the next significant initiative.

The advent of the short video era

While it has subsequently become synonymous with the format, ByteDance was by no means the first company to focus on short videos. The Chinese company Kuaishou Technology had already established a short video platform in 2011, while Vine had been doing the same in the U.S. since 2012. However, during these early years, the product features were quite different from the 15-second short music videos that later proliferated.

In November 2014, Dubsmash made its debut in Germany. As a precursor to lip-syncing video apps like Musical.ly and Douyin, Dubsmash enabled users to create 10-second lip-sync videos based on music and film clips. However, with its lack of social features, Dubsmash soon encountered obstacles. While in subsequent years, video-syncing apps gained traction, they faced challenges in achieving profitability.

China's short video sector started to emerge in 2011, but it took five years before it exploded. By 2016, apps such as Miaopai and Xiaokaxiu were attracting celebrities and bloggers, while Kuaishou was thriving in less urbanized regions in China, particularly in third- and fourth-tier cities. It was within this highly competitive market that ByteDance set out to differentiate itself.

Figure 3   Timeline of short video product releases in China

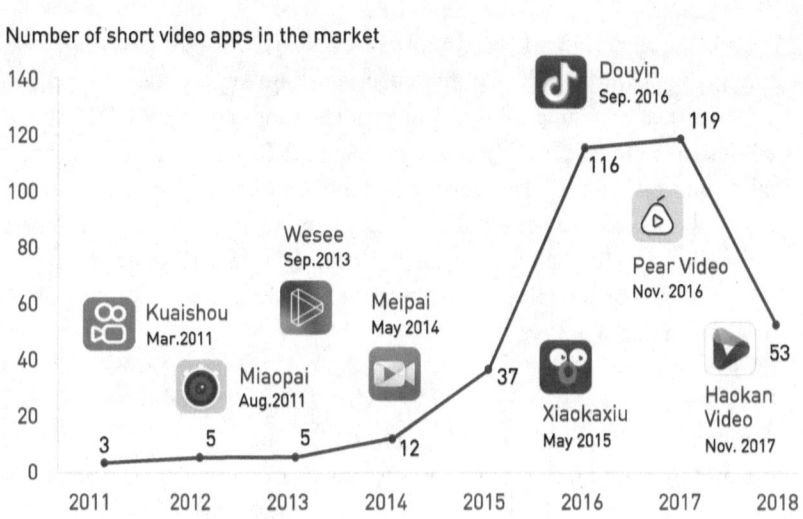

Sources: Cinda Securities, Qimai Data

Douyin rises suddenly

Throughout 2016, ByteDance launched a few different short video applications. In April, Huoshan made its debut, followed by Toutiao Video in May (later renamed Xigua Video), and then in September, A.me (later rebranded as Douyin). Each of these platforms catered to its own target audience and content styles.

Among them, Douyin has gone on to be the best known. The innovative platform, tailored for a youthful audience, revolves around the creation of short music videos. It boasts an extensive library of multimedia resources, enabling users to create their own 15-second musical videos that can be shared with others on the platform.

Douyin was an internal venture of ByteDance. The small founding team of young people, all of whom were Gen Z, focused on generating lifestyle content in areas such as fitness, travel, music, dance, painting and beauty. They established a fashionable and fun style to differentiate themselves from their competitors. In the meantime, the Douyin technical team worked tirelessly to ensure the best possible user experience.

Strategically, ByteDance began to tilt more resources toward Douyin, arming the platform with a cutting-edge algorithm of personal recommendations, supported by a huge advertising campaign. With access to Toutiao's immense traffic base, advertising for Douyin kicked off during the second half of 2017. From around 10 million MAU in June 2017, the numbers doubled to 22.4 million by August and then tripled to a staggering 37.5 million by October. By mid-2019, Douyin's DAU in China had reached 300 million, exceeding its main competitor Kuaishou and remaining well ahead from that point on.

Figure 4   Douyin and Kuaishou MAU

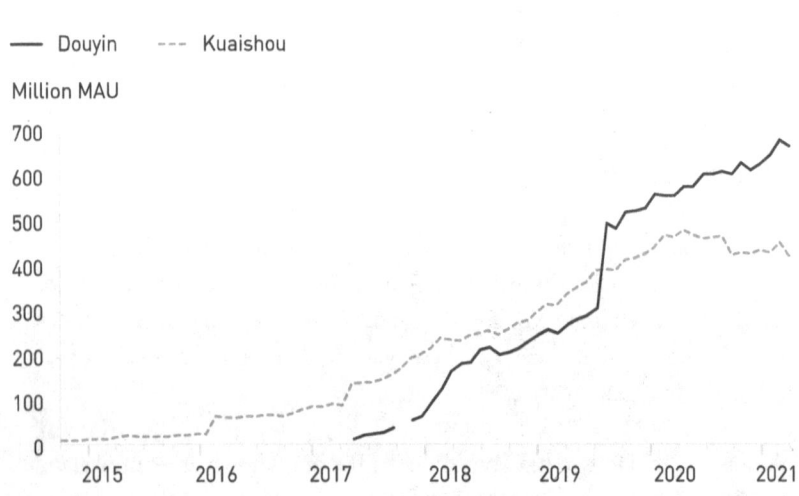

Source: Wind Information

Developing the Douyin business model

Much like its predecessor Toutiao, Douyin built its business model based on its huge number of users. In terms of revenue structure, Douyin mainly relies on two channels. The first, and to date most important income stream, is advertising. Douyin employs two pivotal formats within this category: ads seamlessly woven into videos and customized challenge games that prompt users to complete specific tasks to earn prizes. The second is e-commerce.

Across both Toutiao and Douyin, ByteDance has created two highly efficient commercial operations, with advertising at the heart of the success.

Early in 2019, ByteDance released a new marketing platform "Ocean Engine." According to Zhang Lidong, the ByteDance executive overseeing commercialization, "Our goal is to become the most competitive intelligent advertising and marketing platform globally." It seems that the company is well on target, with ByteDance every year capturing an increasing percentage of China's total internet advertising revenue. In 2020, around USD 30 billion, more than one third (37%) of China's total advertising revenue, was spent on ByteDance platforms. However, while this is a major achievement at the domestic level, in absolute numbers ByteDance's advertising revenue still lags far behind global players, such as Google and Facebook.

Another emerging driver of revenue is e-commerce. Starting in 2019, there has been increasing interest in e-commerce live-streams, which Douyin has tapped into with its own e-commerce platform. During live-streamed videos, information about similar products is introduced via pop-ups. Users can directly purchase through a link or via a third-party platform, from which Douyin takes a percentage of the commission.

Douyin's estimated gross merchandise value (GMV) for 2020 was reported as being more than RMB 500 billion (USD 72.5 billion), three times higher than the previous year. In 2021, Douyin's GMV rose again, reaching RMB 730 billion (USD 113 billion). Douyin achieved this milestone in just two years, a notably quicker pace compared to competitors such as Alibaba, JD.com, and Pinduoduo.

By July 2019, the total global DAU of ByteDance's products exceeded 700 million and the total MAU exceeded 1.5 billion, of which Douyin's DAU alone amounted to 320 million.

By the end of the decade, ByteDance had two key pillars: Toutiao's information distribution services and Douyin's short video services. These two businesses share a similar strategy, namely to attract users to spend more time by satisfying their appetites for information and entertainment and then to capitalize on their engagement through advertising and e-commerce.

ByteDance had left China's other internet giants — Baidu, Alibaba and Tencent — in its wake, to become by far the most popular internet company in China.

TikTok faces the reality of globalization

ByteDance makes international incursions

While Toutiao's earlier international attempt, TopBuzz, had not matched ByteDance's achievements in China, Zhang's ambition for multinational success never faded. He continually sought out overseas opportunities, including a failed attempt to acquire Reddit in 2016.

Based on the successes of Douyin, during 2016 and 2017, ByteDance took steps to enter the global short video market. A critical step was the acquisition of Musical.ly. Founded and launched in the U.S. in 2014 by two Shanghai natives, Alex Zhu and Luyu Yang, by the end of 2017, Musical.ly had 240 million registered users and more than 60 million MAU, most of them based in North America.

Along with various other acquisitions, including Flipagram and LiveMe, ByteDance continued to gain share of the international market through its own self-built video apps. Specifically, from August 2017, ByteDance launched its international version of Douyin, TikTok, in markets including India, Indonesia, Thailand and Japan. Less than a year later, by June 2018, globally TikTok had already attracted more than 150 million DAUs.

Table 1   ByteDance's short video apps

Name	Source	Launch/ acquisition/ investment time	Region	Description
Huoshan	Self-built	April 2016	China	15-second short videos; Targeting lower-tier cities in northern China
Xigua Video	Self-built	May 2016	China	3- to 10-minute videos, similar to YouTube
Douyin	Self-built	September 2016	China	15-second music short videos; Targeting young people, such as university students or young professionals
Buzz Video	Self-built	September 2016	Global	Global version of Xigua Video
Vigo Video	Self-built	July 2017	Indonesia India Thailand Vietnam and others	Global version of Douyin Huoshan
TikTok	Self-built	August 2017	India Indonesia Thailand Japan and others	Global version of Douyin
Flipagram	Acquisition	February 2017	U.S.	Short video social app
Musical.ly	Acquisition	November 2017	North America	Music social video app
Live.me	Investment	November 2017	U.S.	Live-streaming platform

Source: TikTok website

The golden age of TikTok

After acquiring Musical.ly at a cost of USD 1 billion, ByteDance retained its founder Zhu Jun as CEO and leveraged ByteDance's marketing expertise and advanced algorithms to unlock new opportunities. With ByteDance's backing, Musical.ly grew from a pre-acquisition 60 million MAU in November 2017 to 100 million by August 2018.

In August 2018, Musical.ly closed down its operations and merged with TikTok. This move expanded the user experience of TikTok, making it a truly global platform that catered to a wider range of interest groups and operated in more countries and regions. Following the merger, TikTok swiftly rose to become the leading short video app. Meanwhile, Douyin dominated the Chinese market, solidifying ByteDance's position as the absolute leader in the short video sector.

Powered by efficient marketing and algorithms, TikTok experienced astounding success. In 2018, ByteDance launched a major advertising campaign through Facebook, spending USD 1 million per day for more than six months, leading to an immediate surge in downloads. In that year alone, TikTok was downloaded 660 million times, a fourfold increase on 2017.

Figure 5   TikTok global downloads by quarter

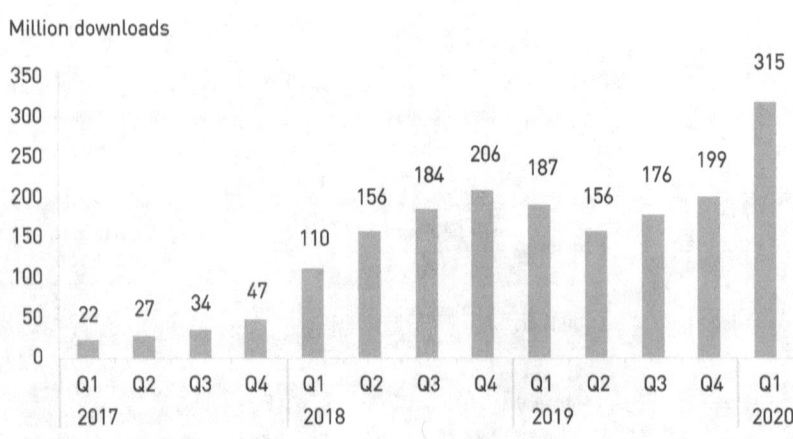

Sources: Cinda Securities, Qimai Data

Early in 2020, with much of the world experiencing COVID-19 related lockdowns and confined to their homes, there was a sudden and unprecedented increased dependence on the internet for entertainment. The short video format swept the globe. Together, Douyin and TikTok rode the wave of success, with 626 million downloads making them the most downloaded apps worldwide in the first half of 2020.

Inevitably, though, the competition intensified. Numerous start-ups entered the short video space and larger internet companies launched short video apps or added short video features to their existing apps. Facebook launched a stand-alone application, Lasso, and later added "Reels" to Instagram. YouTube launched a TikTok-like function, "Shorts" and Snapchat added "Spotlight."

2020: a tough year for TikTok

TikTok has long grappled with challenges concerning user privacy and data security. Starting in 2019 onwards, mounting accusations of security breaches, particularly in key markets such as the U.S. and India led to increasing regulatory measures against ByteDance. The problems escalated, reaching crisis point by mid-2020.

On June 29, 2020, in a move that many believe was precipitated by underlying tensions due to the Sino-Indian border conflict, the Indian Ministry of Electronics and Information Technology announced that it would ban 59 mobile applications developed by Chinese companies, including TikTok.

Meantime, that same year, in the U.S., there were challenges to TikTok in the form of increased scrutiny by the Committee on Foreign Investment in the United States (CFIUS) and various executive orders from then U.S. President Donald Trump.

Table 2 Timeline of U.S. regulatory activities affecting TikTok

August 6, 2020	President Trump signed an executive order announcing that from September 20, he would ban any American individual or company from doing business with ByteDance, WeChat and their subsidiary corporations.
August 14, 2020	The President issued another executive order, requiring ByteDance to divest within 90 days.
August 30, 2020	ByteDance stated that the company would strictly abide by relevant Chinese laws and regulations and handle business related to technology export. Any deal to sell TikTok would likely not go through until after the U.S. elections in November, given the time required for approvals from China.
September 14, 2020	Oracle confirmed that ByteDance had submitted a proposal to the U.S. Treasury Department for Oracle to serve as TikTok's "trusted technology provider." Under this arrangement, TikTok would continue to be based in the U.S., with Oracle acting as the data custodian for TikTok to ensure data security. TikTok would not sell its core algorithms to Oracle.
September 19, 2020	Trump announced that he had approved a cooperation agreement between Oracle, Walmart and TikTok.
September 21, 2020	Trump recanted, saying he would not approve the deal between Oracle and ByteDance if the latter still controlled TikTok. Against the background of the U.S.-China trade tensions, there was less scope for cooperation. Given Trump's capricious attitude, ByteDance decided that suing Trump was its best option.
September 23, 2020	TikTok filed for an emergency federal court hearing in Washington, D.C., requesting to suspend the removal of the app planned for September 27. (It had originally been scheduled for September 20 and later postponed for seven days.) ByteDance officially started the process of litigation.

September 27, 2020	TikTok achieved an initial victory, with Federal Court Judge Carl J. Nichols issuing a preliminary injunction calling a halt to the deliberation about whether to take TikTok offline. After the business turmoil in August and September 2020, TikTok's operations in the U.S. gradually got back on track.
June 9, 2021	New U.S. President, Joseph Biden, revoked the Trump Administration's ban on TikTok and WeChat.
March 23, 2023	TikTok Global CEO Shou Zi Chew was grilled for almost five hours in a hearing of the U.S. House of Representatives. Lawmakers interrogated him about TikTok's ownership, censorship and algorithm, accusing TikTok of being an "enemy of the state."

Source: CKGSB Case Center

Up until mid-2020, Chinese netizens had compared ByteDance with Huawei, referring to it as the pride of Chinese companies going abroad.

However, public opinion in China took a negative turn from July to August 2020 when news broke that ByteDance might be selling TikTok's U.S. operations to a U.S. entity. Zhang faced a dilemma. Trump's executive orders meant the company was facing the existential threat of a U.S. ban, with many of TikTok's American shareholders holding the opinion that the executive order had been precipitated due to a delay in finding a compromise agreement with the U.S. Government. Zhang had continuing ambitions to take his company global, while recognizing the need to protect the integrity of TikTok and ByteDance. Meanwhile, back in China, there was a widespread perception that ByteDance had shown weakness in being too eager to compromise.

ByteDance's TikTok has undoubtedly been one of the most successful global products of modern times, at the forefront of the short video trend, even posing a challenge to Facebook's dominance in social networking. However, Zhang's ambition to go global has faced hurdles, with geo-political issues and the challenges of anti-globalization sometimes overshadowing the growth of his company.

The aftermath

Following on from the events of 2020 and 2021, ByteDance adjusted its overseas strategy. It closed TopBuzz and other less successful overseas products, terminating its international engagement in the news information sector. ByteDance refocused its activity on the short video market, shutting down brands such as Vigo Video and concentrating its resources in order to maximize TikTok's profitability.

In the meantime, ByteDance has been active in various other sectors, such as working on the global expansion of its gaming operations. In March 2021, ByteDance acquired Mutong Technology, whose products rank among the world's top mobile games. The acquisition involved a payment of RMB 10 billion (USD 1.6 billion) in cash and RMB 15 billion (USD 2.3 billion) in stocks, equivalent to a total of USD 3.9 billion.

The future of ByteDance

Looking back at the turmoil of 2020, we can observe how ByteDance's global aspirations suffered setbacks, with the company caught in the crossfire between an impulsive American president and a judgmental Chinese populace. With President Trump threatening to ban TikTok, the same Chinese netizens that had once praised ByteDance as a beacon of Chinese success overseas now perceived the application's potential sale as an act of "surrender" to American hegemony.

Zhang found himself trapped in a predicament: to sell or not to sell. Selling TikTok would have enraged the audience in China; but by holding the line and hanging on to the company, he risked losing out due to the impending prohibition. While some investors felt that Zhang's refusal to compromise had provoked Trump, in China the popular narrative was that Zhang had lost his backbone, with many taking the position that it was better to shut down TikTok altogether rather than sell it.

In summary, TikTok has played a massive role in the development of the short video trend around the globe, giving life to Zhang's dream of globalization driven by internet entrepreneurship and enterprise. Yet, as is the case with many multinationals, recent growth has been hampered by the trend toward de-globalization, driven and fueled by local political agendas.

Updates

- Following a two-year hiatus and period of relative calm, ByteDance has once again been up against the U.S. regulators in 2023, with some lawmakers for both parties now pushing for the sale of ByteDance.

- It was reported in September 2023 that ByteDance and the U.S. government are seeking to find a middle ground for TikTok's fate.

- Overseas revenue reportedly doubled during 2022, while domestic revenue growth has slowed, up by 25% YoY.

- TikTok had 1.4 billion MAU in 2022 and is expected to reach 1.8 billion by the end of 2023. It is reportedly working toward launching a full-service e-commerce business in the U.S., aiming to replicate the success of shopping platforms such as SHEIN and Temu.

- An initial public offering for ByteDance has been highly anticipated for years, but the company has said since 2021 it had no imminent plans for an IPO.

Banking on Data
MYbank's Innovation in Supply Chain Finance

Song Zhongzhi, Associate Professor of Finance, Shanghai Jiao Tong University; Former Assistant Professor of Finance, Cheung Kong Graduate School of Business

Li Mengjun, Senior Researcher, Case Center, Cheung Kong Graduate School of Business

China's private sector, which primarily comprises micro-, small- and medium-sized enterprises (MSMEs), is the backbone of the Chinese economy. It contributes more than 50% of tax revenue, more than 60% of GDP, more than 70% of technological innovations, more than 80% of urban employment and more than 90% of market entities in China. MSMEs play a pivotal role in driving economic growth, but with conventional commercial banks in China tending to be risk-averse, MSMEs often face difficulties obtaining cheap financing due to a lack of credit and collateral.

In the past, MSMEs often relied heavily on "core enterprises" for credit. These core enterprises are key players in the supply chain, coordinating and driving the flow of goods, service and payments. Typically large-scale buyers and manufacturers, they have enormous power stemming from their ability to set payment terms and conditions for their suppliers.

To address the challenge of providing credit to MSMEs, MYbank, an Alibaba-backed digital bank in China, launched a finance system named the "Goose System."

Money talks: introducing MYbank

MYbank was established by Alibaba's affiliate firm Ant Group in June 2015 and from the outset has positioned itself as a digital financing institution serving MSMEs and individuals with limited access to bank financing. MYbank operates without brick-and-mortar branches, instead aiming to be a technology-based online bank.

MSMEs often require quick and flexible access to low-interest loans. However, their sometimes limited collateral, sparse credit records and incomplete financial reports may make them less appealing to traditional lenders, even for relatively small loan amounts.

In its early days, MYbank mainly served e-commerce sellers on Taobao and Tmall. By leveraging transaction data accumulated on these e-commerce platforms, the company developed a unique big-data automated loan processing system that was referred to as "310," since it granted loans within three minutes and disbursed them in one second with zero human intervention. Since 2017, MYbank has expanded its online lending to serving offline businesses using a QR-code-based payment system, through which it has achieved solid cashflow and has served MSMEs and individual businesses in sectors including retail, catering, clothing, logistics, construction and manufacturing.

At present, MYbank has three major business units, providing finance services for MSMEs, rural communities and supply chains respectively. As of the end of 2022, MYbank had served more than 50 million small- and micro-level customers. For 80% of its clients, MYbank is their first business loan provider.

Branching out: Why focus on supply chain finance?

In 2016, Alibaba announced that it would be focusing on "new retail" and "new finance." Backed by Ant Group, MYbank responded by launching "self-factoring" for Tmall brand owners, a service that allowed Tmall sellers to receive early payments for invoices that had yet to be paid. MYbank subsequently extended its services to offering loans to eligible distributors and companies operating within the Alibaba-supported supply chains of the Cainiao logistics and Hema retail services.

In 2018, MYbank made the move to operate beyond Alibaba's e-commerce ecosystem. There were several reasons behind this decision.

- MYbank has a mission to empower as many MSMEs as possible across society, by providing them with convenient and affordable financial services. In 2018, outside of Alibaba's e-commerce ecosystem, there were a further 20 million small- and micro-scale enterprises, 60 million individually-owned businesses, as well as an unknown but significant number of unlicensed individual operators that were being underserved.
- Many core enterprises, or large corporations such as Mengniu (a dairy company) and Liby (a detergent manufacturer), reached out to MYbank to provide supply chain financial services for their downstream and upstream MSME partners.
- Through its operation within the confines of Alibaba, MYbank accumulated large volumes of data, an understanding of risk management and experience in granting credit and offering interest rate concessions, all based on the dynamic needs of merchants. This knowledge and experience was available to extend to a broader set of customers beyond Alibaba.

Don't break the bank: obstacles in traditional supply chain finance

Conventional financial institutions have tended to focus on providing supply chain financial services to core enterprises and their upstream suppliers, leaving businesses on the downstream of the industrial chain with less access to financing. Surveys had shown that more than 70% of distributors were short of funding and in need of financial support to grow their businesses.

In the eyes of traditional financial institutions, it is difficult to rate the credit worthiness of a downstream enterprise purely on the basis of the core enterprises it serves. It is all the more challenging when the distribution network comprises a large number of outlets.

Additionally, the competitiveness, sales and solvency of distributors may be compromised if they procure from a single core enterprise. Financial institutions will not necessarily offer credit to a distributor solely on the basis that they sell an established brand; at the same time, it is simply not feasible to assess a distributor's credit-worthiness on a one-by-one basis.

However, small- and micro-sized businesses and distributors invariably make up the bulk of a well-developed distribution network and hence play a vital role in ensuring the success of the large core enterprises with which they work.

The Goose System: innovating the supply chain finance model

MYbank recognized that the methods used by conventional banks to assess the risk of default were not appropriate for these MSME borrowers and that it needed to find a new way to evaluate applications for credit. As part of Alibaba's internet empire, it could draw on the technology company's experience and capability of working in the digital economy. Therefore, MYbank developed an integrated digital supply chain finance solution, the "Goose System," in collaboration with tech teams from Alibaba Cloud and DingTalk, an Alibaba communication platform.

The Goose System is essentially a digital transaction monitoring platform, centered on core enterprises but covering businesses along the entire supply chain.

Alibaba serves companies large and small, generating abundant data. With access to the data, MYbank can assess how well these companies are performing. Thus, similar to how it analyzes QR code payments to assess small businesses, MYbank has access to a reliable information source to verify a borrower's credit level when both parties to a transaction are using the Goose System. Based on the data acquired, MYbank offers a range of cloud debt products covering different stages of supply chain finance for businesses of varying sizes.

The Goose System requires no collateral and runs without human intervention. It can span the entire supply chain and now extends across China. Currently, more than 500 large brands, or core enterprises, including Haier (home appliances), Huawei (electronics), Mengniu (dairy) and Want Want (food and beverage), have adopted the system. MSMEs, and in particular those that are their distributors, now have an alternative basis for their "credit rating," i.e., their transaction data with these core companies, making them eligible for credit loans. Thanks to the Goose System, MSMEs face a much lower barrier than they had previously confronted when accessing traditional supply chain finance. Almost 80% of core enterprises' downstream distributors and brick-and-mortar stores now have access to business loans. With its large data pool, the Goose System has been able to analyze combined transaction data across different supply chains that had previously been assumed to be irrelevant to one another and in doing so has been able to more clearly map out various markets and industries. The more data MYbank can acquire, the better its chances of creating a novel and successful method of risk management, something that cannot be matched by a traditional bank.

While traditional supply chain financial services have tended to favor large-scale businesses, the Goose System has meant there is now loan coverage for all distributors, especially the medium- and small-sized ones. The approval rate of business loans for MSMEs through Goose is currently running higher than 80%. It has particularly benefitted China's under-developed regions, with nearly half the SMEs using MYbank's procurement loan services being located in central and western China. The Goose System and its digital credit have also alleviated the need for core enterprises to vouch for their distributors, thereby minimizing their exposure to financial risk.

Figure 1 Goose system product matrix

Source: MYbank 2022 sustainability report

Take that to the bank

Providing digital solutions to supply chains

Mengniu provides an example of how MYbank can work in the real world. The Chinese dairy giant has almost 20,000 distributors in China, between them covering more than 1.3 million stores. These downstream distributors have previously experienced difficulty securing loans. As early as 2009, Mengniu started trying to address this barrier, working with financial institutions to provide financing services to downstream distributors. However, loans were only provided to the largest distributors — those with sales exceeding RMB 10 million (USD 1.5 million) — leaving the remaining 70% of distributors without access to credit.

In 2018, MYbank began providing exclusive procurement loan services to Mengniu's downstream small- and medium-sized distributors. The service has outperformed Mengniu's expectations. Since partnering with MYbank, the approval rate of business loans for Mengniu's downstream distributors has risen to 80%, 58% of them coming from the under-developed central and western regions of China. According to Mengniu's supply chain financing platform, distributors using MYbank's digital financial services in 2020 saw a 22% YoY growth in sales volume, compared with only 10% for those who did not use MYbank.

As well as offering loans to distributors, MYbank's Goose System also addresses the difficulties of fund management through its "cloud fund" offering, as illustrated in Figure 1.

MYbank provides firms with a complete set of online payment and fund management tools, including cash registers, account distribution, purchase payment collection and so on. Having these various functions under one single system simplifies account reconciliation, reduces costs, ensures compliance and ultimately improves efficiency of enterprise fund management.

In 2021, Happy Sweet Potato, a Chinese tea chain with nearly 2,000 franchise stores nationwide, combined its business and funds management systems using MYbank's Goose System. The system has allowed Happy Sweet Potato to accurately identify the source of payments in its offline stores and to automatically record accounts in the system, thereby enabling headquarters to immediately dispatch goods as soon as a franchise store has paid for them. Financial efficiency has increased by 30% compared with the earlier set-up, in which accounts were cross-checked across multiple systems.

In summary, the Goose System has achieved success as a digitalized solution for supply chains, bringing with it enormous positive externalities.

Cash strapped: the challenges it faces

MYbank has, however, faced challenges with the Goose System.

Challenge 1: understanding the subtleties of different businesses

MYbank's supply chain finance team is primarily focused on finance and therefore may not be familiar with the differing needs of specific business sectors. In order to fully serve SMEs in the supply chain, MYbank needs to better understand the specific demands of core enterprises and meet these requirements.

To date, MYbank has served 500 core enterprises in nearly 20 industries. It takes time to build up an understanding of each industry, its underlying structure and any idiosyncrasies. Similarly, there may be regional differences, local policies and seasonal changes to be taken into account. MYbank needs to be sufficiently flexible to be able to adapt to these different situations, rather than taking a "one size fits all" approach.

Challenge 2: obstacles associated with core enterprise customers

Another set of major challenges for MYbank is the technological barriers that eventuate from core enterprises that are not yet digitally advanced. While MYbank has been in contact with more than 1,000 core enterprises, over 80% of them lack the required digital capacity to access the Goose System. Of concern, many appear to be lacking the motivation to digitalize, since doing so will require a high level of upfront investment, with the benefits not immediately apparent.

If core enterprises are not digitalized, the quality data required for accurate risk assessment will not be available to MYbank, stymieing the opportunity for loan issuance.

To overcome these barriers, MYbank is working closely with Ant Group to try to encourage core enterprises to reach an adequate level of digitalization.

MYbank is currently focused on expanding its B2B business in supply chain finance, which brings with it many challenges. B2B business is non-standardized and requires significant business development resources. To issue loans to small and micro enterprises in the supply chain requires MYbank to obtain data from core enterprises. Challenges arise if these core enterprises are unwilling, for whatever reason, to cooperate with MYbank.

Another issue is that some core enterprises have requested commissions from the finance that MYbank has provided to their suppliers and distributors. MYbank has been reluctant to enter into these kinds of transactions, since it will inevitably involve transferring the cost burden onto the small- and micro-sized enterprises, increasing the financial pressure on them at a time when regulatory departments have been encouraging financial institutions to provide credit to MSMEs at lower interest rates.

Challenge 3: promoting MYbank

While the model may be highly functional, MYbank has been lacking a dedicated sales force to promote its services. By contrast, most of MYbank's conventional commercial bank competitors have a large network of branches, numerous client managers and an established presence in the industry.

Ever since it was established, MYbank has acknowledged that it would not compete head-on with traditional financial institutions. Instead, MYbank has set out to collaborate with these banks, to share and co-develop the market, offering them improved operational efficiency through MYbank's fintech technology.

Conventional banks certainly have the advantage when it comes to managing people, while the data-driven MYbank excels at processing data. Any cooperation between the two is win-win: banks are able to make more deals and MYbank earns a commission fee for each loan.

A bank you can bank on: the future of MYbank

The COVID-19 pandemic accelerated demand for contactless financial services, providing a clear advantage to online banks. Data and information have been key to the development of finance for those smaller supply chain enterprises that were not being well served by the traditional financial institutions. However, there are considerable risks in data acquisition and use. MYbank will need to ensure that data security is uppermost, in order to minimize the risks to its business operations and to ensure compliance with regulatory authorities.

The MYbank 2022 Sustainability Report clearly outlines its positioning, as "an explorer of internet banking and a practitioner of inclusive finance." MYbank has worked to solve the problems associated with microfinance through the use of technology, assisting MSMEs by providing efficient and convenient financial services. Further, it has taken an open and cooperative partnership approach in its dealings with traditional banks, local governments, tax bureaus and financing guarantee companies.

Rather than focusing solely on economic returns, MYbank has prioritized the social value generated through its businesses. MYbank needs to continue to ensure that it takes the necessary safeguards to minimize market, credit and operational risks, while improving profitability and ensuring healthy development in the long run through championing innovative approaches to fintech.

Updates

- Despite a rise in its nonperforming loan ratio in 2022, due to measures taken to help MSMEs offset the impact of the COVID-19 pandemic, MYbank still posted higher profits and healthy liquidity metrics for the year.

- Growth in total assets slowed during 2022, up only 10% compared with a 26% rise the previous year.

- MYbank continues to innovate and expand its product offerings, launching a product in 2022 offering MSMEs a credit line of up to RMB 5 million (USD 744,000) that can be used for working capital, capital expenditures and other business needs.

Chapter Two

Changing Industrial Supply Chains

China's supply chains have evolved through both large-scale manufacturing and innovative technological ecosystems, supported by strategic governmental policies, investments in R&D and an emphasis on international trade and cooperation. This section provides an investigation into Chinese companies that are reshaping the conventional landscape, not only in China but also on a global scale. NIO demonstrates the powerful effect of technology investments and original equipment manufacturer partnerships. Linglong Tire showcases the disruptive impact of digitalization on traditional business models. And TCL illustrates the opportunities that arise from vertical integration and strategic acquisitions.

Case Studies

4 Steering Toward Success?
NIO's First 10 Years as an EV Upstart

5 Rolling Forward
The Evolution of Linglong Tire

6 Powering Ahead
How TCL Transformed and Upgraded

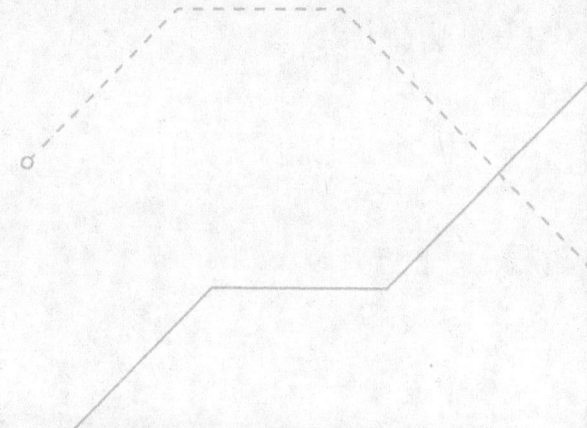

Steering Toward Success?
NIO's First 10 Years as an EV Upstart

Li Wei, Professor of Economics, Associate Dean for Asia and Director of the Case Center, Cheung Kong Graduate School of Business

Zhu Yunhai, Researcher, Case Center, Cheung Kong Graduate School of Business

The year 2022 saw a massive expansion in the electric vehicle (EV) industry in China. While the COVID-19 pandemic had a detrimental effect on many other sectors in the economy, growth in the EV industry at that time soared. Data from the China Association of Automobile Manufacturers indicates that total automobile sales in China reached 26.9 million units, a YoY increase of 2.1%. Of these, around one quarter (6.9 million units) were electric vehicles, a 93% increase in sales on the previous year. There is every expectation that this rapid growth will continue for years to come.

One of China's better-known EV manufacturers, NIO, delivered 122,486 vehicles in 2022, a YoY increase of 34%. That year, Xpeng Motors delivered 120,757 vehicles, a 23% YoY increase, and Li Auto delivered 133,246, a 47% increase. For NIO and, more generally, for China's EV sector, rising sales and rapid market expansion signify that a new era has dawned.

Despite being a relative latecomer to the automotive industry, NIO has quickly overtaken many of the established players. As of March 2023, NIO ranked as the world's fourth largest EV company in terms of market capitalization, behind Tesla, Li Auto and Lucid Motors.

What are the possible next steps in NIO's development strategy? Could NIO replicate Tesla's success in China? How will the company ensure its future in China's increasingly competitive EV market?

Hitting the road

A brief history of NIO

Established in November 2014, NIO was one of the earliest Chinese EV companies to base its R&D, product and sales upon an "internet mindset." In contrast with more traditional automobile manufacturers, during its early years, NIO initially focused strongly on building brand recognition, rather than developing products or constructing a sales network.

NIO's first ground-breaking achievement was to win the 2014–2015 Formula E Championship, making it the first-ever Chinese team to win a driver championship at an FIA event. At this point, NIO did not have a mass-produced car, but the achievement helped raise brand recognition.

NIO subsequently expanded its operations by constructing its headquarters in Shanghai and establishing branch offices worldwide. In November 2016, the company launched its English brand name, "NIO," and showcased its supercar model, the EP9, in London. The sports car would go on to set a new lap record for an electric vehicle at the German Nürburgring Nordschleife circuit, confirming its status as the world's fastest electric car. In December 2017, NIO officially released its first mass-produced car, the ES8. From then on, NIO's business continued to expand. By 2022, NIO had 26,763 full-time employees.

Today, the company has set up research and development centers around the world, including in Shanghai (production models), Beijing (software), San Jose (intelligent driving) and Oxford (advanced engineering), as well as a global design center in Munich. In cities such as Oslo, NIO provides a full product and service experience at NIO Houses, its customer experience centers around the world.

Figure 1   NIO's global deployment

Source: NIO website

Investors and core management team

NIO's founder and Chairman, William Li, is often referred to in China as being the "godfather of the transport sector." In 2000, Li co-founded Beijing Bitauto E-Commerce, where he served as Director and President until 2006. From 2010 to 2020, he served as Chair at Bitauto Holdings Limited, a NYSE-listed automobile service company and a leading automobile service provider in China.

NIO's early shareholders included many well-known companies and investment institutions, such as Tencent, Baidu, Smart Group (an investment entity of Richard Liu, founder of JD.com), Hillhouse Capital and Sequoia Capital.

Right from the start, NIO pulled together a highly experienced core management team that included former top executives of major players such as Tesla, BMW, Volkswagen, General Motors and Guangzhou Automobile Company (GAC).

With this combination of a strong management team and prominent investors, NIO was able to undergo rapid development, transitioning from prototype to mass production within just a few years.

The path toward mass production

NIO's debut electric vehicle, the EP9 sports car, hit the market in November 2016, with a starting price of USD 1.48 million. It was not sold to the general public, instead only being made available to a small number of high-profile investors and shareholders, such as Tencent's Pony Ma, JD.com's Richard Liu and Xiaomi's Lei Jun. This marketing strategy helped establish NIO as a premium brand in the electric vehicle market.

The company subsequently rolled out its first mass-produced electric vehicle, the ES8, in December 2017, with a base price in China of RMB 448,000 (USD 66,370). Targeted at the mid-to-high-end SUV market, the ES8 was well received, proving NIO's capacity to produce electric vehicles on a mass scale. The company went on to unveil several affordable electric cars, such as the mid-size luxury SUV ES6 (RMB 368,000, USD 54,700).

NIO's initial public offering

NIO's initial public offering (IPO) on the NYSE in September 2018 was a significant milestone for the company. Shares were priced at USD 6.26, and the company ended up raising about USD 1 billion, the third largest amount in history for a Chinese company in the U.S., after Alibaba and iQiyi. The company's market capitalization at that time was at over USD 6 billion.

Despite the success of the IPO, many overseas investors remained skeptical about NIO's long-term prospects. Analysts at Bloomberg had NIO pegged as a high-risk investment in its article entitled "Shame, Tesla-alike NIO Could Have Used the Extra Cash." Their predictions were proven correct when, in November 2019, NIO's shares plummeted to USD 1.45. The company then went on to make an astounding comeback in 2020, with the stock rebounding to USD 60 per share. At one point NIO's market value rose to over USD 100 billion, more than ten times what it had been at its IPO.

The three pillars of NIO's core competitiveness

NIO's emergence as a major player in China's electric vehicle sector is a testament to its skill at navigating the challenges of the industry, through the company's innovative approach to production, product positioning, brand promotion, sales model and customer service. All of these have contributed to its core competitiveness and success to date.

1. Reducing costs through original equipment manufacturing

One of the key drivers of NIO's success has been its ability to keep costs down through its original equipment manufacturer production model.

In traditional automobile manufacturing, significant investment input is initially required to secure land, build factories and acquire equipment. As a start-up, NIO was not able to bear the high costs of this heavy-asset model.

At the time of NIO's inception, the petrol-powered automobile market had become saturated and many automakers were encumbered with idle production lines. Recognizing this opportunity, NIO took an asset-light approach, outsourcing all production to a Chinese vehicle manufacturer, JAC Motors.

NIO's relationship with JAC Motors has been collaborative. JAC Motors owns the production plants, equipment, assembly lines and factory personnel while NIO oversees the entire process of production, quality control and inspection standards. NIO also collaborates with JAC Motors on research and testing. Through this model, NIO has been able to ramp up its production capacity. In the nearly three years from May 2018 to April 2022, NIO produced 100,000 vehicles, a record number for the high-end SUV market.

There was some speculation as to whether NIO would be able to construct its own production base, given the sales volume. For a short time, NIO had intended to build a factory in Shanghai. However, these plans were shelved in 2019 when the company decided instead to continue its collaboration with JAC Motors. This involved various efforts, including forming a joint venture in 2021 to jointly manufacture NIO cars.

2. Spearheading technology: vehicle OS and auto driving capability

NIO's tech integration efforts are focused on two key aspects: its vehicle operation system (OS) and autonomous driving.

The NIO vehicle OS, named "NOMI," is the world's first in-vehicle operating system powered by a cloud-computing platform. Passengers are able to use verbal commands to carry out various functions, such as adjusting seating and altering the vehicle temperature. Users have generally been very positive in their reviews of the NOMI system, noting that the thrill of using NOMI is akin to saying "Hello Siri" for the first time.

The technology used in autonomous driving can be broadly divided into two categories: light detection and ranging (LiDAR) systems, as used by Huawei, and those based on camera technology, as used in Tesla's vehicles.

NIO took a pragmatic approach, adopting both technologies when building its Aquila Super Sensing system. Launched in early 2021 and used in NIO's first autonomous driving model, the ET7, the Aquila system features 33 high-performance sensing units, which include eleven 8-megapixel high-resolution cameras, one ultralong-range high-resolution LiDAR, five millimeter-wave radars, twelve ultrasonic sensors and two high-precision positioning units. In terms of types and number of sensors used, NIO's Aquila system far outperforms those of its competitors, including Xpeng and Tesla.

NIO's vehicles are powered by the NIO Adam supercomputer, which is built using four NVIDIA DIVE Orin systems-on-a-chip (SoC), providing more than 1,000 TOPS of performance.

3. Personalized services

NIO has further differentiated itself from traditional automobile companies by implementing a self-operated direct sales model, similar to Tesla's "offline experience store + online direct sales" strategy.

Consumers interested in NIO can learn about its products, services and prices from NIO's website or mobile app. Armed with a basic understanding of NIO's offerings, they are then invited to one of NIO's stores for a more in-depth physical experience, which might include a test drive. Customers then return online to complete the purchasing process, at which point they can choose their vehicle configurations and apply for financial services.

Unlike the traditional dealer system, where vehicle delivery marks the end of the manufacturer's responsibility, NIO continues its engagement post-purchase, offering a range of services, such as battery charging, maintenance, repair and various membership activities. By eliminating dealers as intermediaries, NIO has been able to significantly save costs and to establish a direct communication channel with customers, which allows it to rapidly acquire feedback from customers and the market in general.

NIO's commitment to providing a unique user experience is evident in its heavy investment in branding and experiential infrastructure. It has constructed a network of "NIO Houses" in the heart of major cities all over China and beyond. These are often very large facilities and serve not only as product showcases, but also as communities for car owners to socialize with one another. The spaces are available to use for lectures, forums and even children's birthday parties.

In 2022 alone, NIO opened 63 new NIO Houses, 79 "NIO Spaces" (vehicle display rooms), 101 service centers and 25 delivery centers around the world. This brings NIO's global sales and services network to 99 NIO Houses, 303 NIO Spaces, 288 service centers and 48 delivery centers.

NIO has also made significant strides in energy infrastructure. The company added 538 new battery-swapping stations worldwide in 2022, making a total of 1,315. Other than that, NIO has China's largest nationwide network of charging piles, with a total of 13,384. Most of these charging and swapping facilities are available to NIO owners for free or at a heavily discounted price.

In summary, NIO presents itself as more than a car manufacturer: it is also a service provider and a membership club. It provides a range of services with the aim of maximizing positive connections between the brand and its customers. In doing so, NIO hopes to differentiate the brand and build loyalty within an industry brimming with competitors.

Applying the brakes? NIO's challenges

Even with the challenges arising from the COVID-19 pandemic, NIO managed to maintain stable deliveries during 2022. However, internal and external stakeholders within the automobile industry and capital markets have varying views on the future prospects of EV makers like NIO.

Can NIO achieve net profitability?

NIO's immediate challenge is to achieve short-term operating profitability within an environment of cut-throat competition among the increasing number of domestic and overseas EV players.

NIO's total revenue in 2022 amounted to RMB 49.27 billion (USD 7.3 billion), a YoY increase of 36%. Despite the increase, the company suffered a significant net loss of RMB 14.44 billion (USD 2.2 billion) for the year. By the end of 2022, NIO had RMB 23.04 billion (USD 3.4 billion) in cash reserves against total assets of RMB 96.26 billion (USD 14.3 billion) and total liabilities of RMB 68.62 billion (USD 10.2 billion).

Even with significant revenue growth and ample cash reserves, NIO has yet to turn a net profit. While a certain degree of loss is acceptable for a newly-established business, there will come a time — some would say it has already arrived — when stakeholders will expect NIO to attain profitability at the operational level. Hence, NIO needs to work out how to address its cost structure and to increase production efficiency.

How long can NIO's competitive advantage continue?

As the EV market continues to grow, so will the level of competition. Inevitably, only a small number of companies will survive. Does NIO have the core capabilities to be among the chosen few?

Thus far, NIO has gained a competitive edge in the EV market through its exceptional service. Its personalized "butler" services have enhanced the overall user experience and helped built a fervently loyal customer base. But these types of premium services come at a cost. The annual operating cost of running NIO Houses in China's first-tier cities is around RMB 100 million (USD 14.9 million). Further, NIO's capacity to offer premium, personalized services is likely to dwindle as car sales rise. One of the major challenges for NIO will be to continue to offer its high-quality services while keeping operating costs down.

In terms of technology accumulation, NIO is still running behind major EV players like BYD and Tesla. While NIO's software systems are popular among its customers, to get ahead in the technologically-advanced EV sector requires more than advanced vehicle OS and auto-driving capability. With the rise of NIO cars on the road, there have been several serious on-road incidents, which have impacted perceptions of the NIO brand.

NIO under heightened competition

Interestingly, NIO's product roadmap and strategic plan identify Mercedes, BMW and Audi as its core competitors. At the ET7 launch event, NIO indicated that the ET7 would be competing with the BMW 7 Series and Apple's upcoming electric car. While NIO claims not to be directly competing with Tesla, the world's most valuable EV company is unquestionably a rival in China's EV market. Both NIO and Tesla first entered the automotive industry with luxury car offerings, but while Tesla has since found success in the mass market with its Model 3, NIO has remained focused on the luxury electric vehicle segment. However, the launch of the ET7 does suggest that NIO is looking to service a broader market segment.

NIO falls well behind Tesla in terms of production capacity and sales. With the move to localize its production in China, Tesla has seen its sales skyrocket. This has enabled the company to reduce the price of its Model Y by RMB 100,000 (USD 14,870), dealing a significant blow to many Chinese domestic EV companies.

To achieve its future development goals, NIO has set its sights on expanding into various overseas markets. It has set up offices in the United States, the United Kingdom and Germany. NIO launched in Norway in 2021 and ventured into Germany, the Netherlands, Denmark, and Sweden in October 2022. The United States and Europe are both important markets for electric vehicle companies, but the competition there is also fierce. There is no doubt, to achieve success and profitability on the global stage, NIO will need to invest considerable effort and resources.

 **Updates**

- NIO delivered 19,329 vehicles in August 2023, increasing by 81% YoY.

- With a mostly new or totally overhauled line up, NIO vehicle prices have dropped following an EV price war in China.

- A planned expansion into Europe based on a new line up of affordable compact cars will reportedly be sold under a different brand name. In the meantime, the European Commission has announced an anti-subsidy probe into Chinese EVs.

- In October 2023, NIO announced plans to cut 10% of "duplicate" and "inefficient" staff roles. Project investment that will not contribute to the company's financial performance within three years will be deferred or discontinued.

- NIO has been diversifying into other sectors, including insurance and mobile phones.

Rolling Forward
The Evolution of Linglong Tire

Teng Bingsheng, Professor of Strategic Management and Associate Dean for Strategic Research, Cheung Kong Graduate School of Business

Wang Xiaolong, Senior Researcher, Case Center, Cheung Kong Graduate School of Business

Inextricably connected to the modern world, the tire has played a vital role in the development of modern transport. With its origins in the 19th century, the tire as we know is a result of ongoing and gradual improvements. Many of the early tire companies, such as Dunlop and Michelin, still remain as key players. Within this environment, how might an emerging Chinese tire company innovate its retail strategy so as to compete with global champions?

The tire industry is a massive business, playing a significant role in the automobile ecosystem. According to the industry publication *Tire Business*, in 2019, global tire market sales amounted to around USD 167 billion. The world's three largest "first-tier" players held 38% market share at that time: Michelin and Bridgestone each held 15% and Goodyear had 8%. This was, however, a decline from 1998 when the same three leaders had held 55% market share between them, an indication of the increasing competition within the market over the twenty-year period.

Over the past decade, among the top 75 global tire brands, the market share held by Chinese tire companies has been gradually increasing, up from

31% in 2015 to 36% in 2019. The COVID-19 pandemic is likely to have accelerated a shift in the market toward China, as tire companies elsewhere in the world suffered heavy losses due to production shutdowns.

The rubber hits the road

Linglong Tire's first forty years

In the earliest days of China's reform and opening-up era, as the economy grew, but before China had developed its own production capacity, tires were a veritable "black gold" due to increasing demand and a shortage of local supply. Smugglers used fishing boats to transport tires from Hong Kong to Shenzhen. Another method of bringing in this valuable contraband was to drive a dual-licensed SUV between the two cities, going back and forth all day, bringing in five new tires per trip, four on the wheels and one as the spare.

Linglong Tire (or "Linglong") has a history that precedes the reform and opening-up period. Starting as the Zhaoyuan Tire Repair Plant in 1975, within forty years Linglong was listed on the main board of the Shanghai Stock Exchange in July 2016. Having undergone several changes in the equity ownership of the business and periods of restructuring, Linglong Tire is now one of China's leading tire manufacturers, with well-established domestic and international production facilities and sales networks. In 2020, Linglong had the largest output of semi-steel and radial tires in China and the highest total profit. According to the 2021 ranking of global tire makers in the UK-based magazine *Tyrepress*, Linglong Tire ranked twelfth by revenue.

Linglong Tire mainly engages in the design, development, manufacturing and sale of tires for passenger, commercial and construction vehicles. Around the world, it has seven production bases — five in China, one in Serbia and another in Thailand — as well as seven R&D institutes across China, the U.S. and Germany.

Linglong sold more than 63 million tires worldwide in 2020, and expects to be rolling out 120 million tires a year by 2025. By 2030, its total annual capacity is forecast to increase to 160 million, which would rank the company as the fifth largest in the world.

In terms of branding, Linglong has adopted a diversified strategy, with differentiated sales campaigns conducted across the world. Its main brands are Linglong, Leao, ATLAS and EVOLUXX, and its products are sold in 173 countries. Its branding slogan is, "Seven of the top ten car companies in the world choose Linglong tires."

As shown in Figure 1, Linglong's operating income grew from RMB 8.73 billion (USD 1.4 billion) in 2015 to RMB 18.38 billion (USD 2.7 billion) in 2020, equivalent to a compound annual growth rate of 16%.

Figure 1   Linglong Tire's operating income and YoY growth

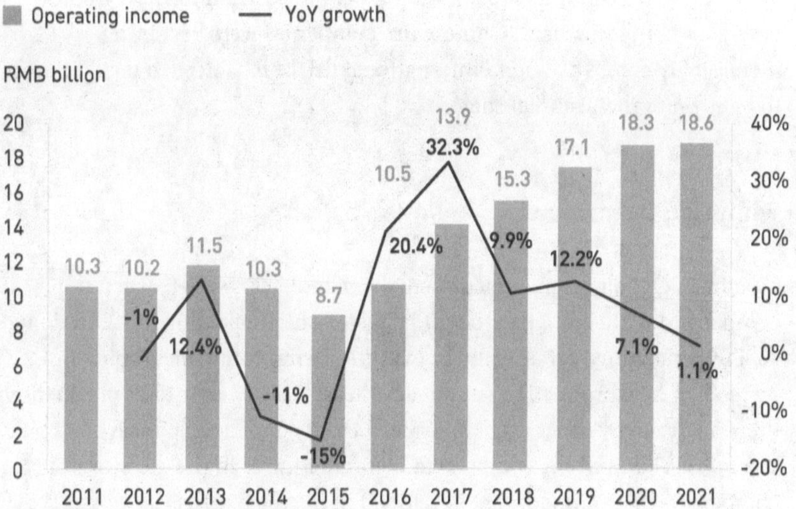

Sources: Linglong annual reports, Sinolink Securities

Navigating the trade barrier

While not the first time that import duties had been imposed on Chinese tires coming into the U.S., 2015 marked a turning point when a general tax of 87.99% and an individual tax of 25.30% were levied on Chinese tire imports by the U.S. Department of Commerce. The number of passenger car tires exported from China to the United States collapsed from 50.4 million in 2014 to 2.8 million in 2019, an almost 95% decline. The impact is reflected in Figure 1 in Linglong's operating income, which actually shrank by 15% in 2015.

With the introduction of the "anti-dumping and subsidy" sanctions on passenger car tires, many Chinese tire companies switched their focus instead to exporting truck and bus tires to the U.S. market. However, the opportunities in this segment were short-lived. As the trade war between the U.S. and China heated up in 2019, further restrictions were imposed, leading to a 65% plunge in truck tire exports from China to the U.S., from 9.2 million in 2018 to 3.2 million in 2019.

While there were multiple factors at play in the decision to apply import taxes, one thing was clear: Chinese tire companies were becoming increasingly competitive and international tire brands needed tariff barriers to hang on to their market share.

Venturing Overseas

Linglong's globalization strategy actually dates back to 2010, when the company took the initiative to build a factory in Thailand in 2012. In doing so, Linglong joined other Chinese manufacturing companies "going out," by seeding new production sites in Southeast Asia, so as to shift production there and thereby offset exchange rate volatility and avoid punitive tariffs. This allowed the company to be more nimble in the deteriorating competitive environment that developed in the mid-2010s.

Today, overseas factories contribute most of the net profits to Chinese domestic tire companies and their profit margins far exceed those of domestic factories. In fact, by 2020, Linglong's overseas factories contributed more than 70% of its net profit.

The problem of tariffs has been just one of a host of issues facing China's tire makers over the past decade. They have also had to deal with regulations regarding environmental protection, fluctuations in the prices of raw materials and, more recently, the dramatic curveball of the COVID-19 pandemic.

Faced with the difficulties in operating conditions, the industry in China has undergone supply-side structural reform, pushing firms to increase production efficiency, which has had the effect of sifting out weaker producers. Each year since 2016, the number of tire producers in China has been declining. In Shandong province alone, 65 tire companies with a previous annual output of 17.32 million bias tires stopped production during 2020. With the consolidation of the market came a smaller, more concentrated group of market leaders.

More generally, over the past ten years, the structure of the global tire industry has undergone changes. The net profits of overseas tire giants have dropped sharply, while the net profit rates of Chinese enterprises have increased. The impact of the COVID-19 pandemic intensified the cost pressures for overseas tire companies, with factories all around the world forced to suspend production, with profits dwindling as a result. In 2020, Goodyear and Bridgestone lost USD 1.3 billion and USD 219 million respectively.

Meanwhile, in China, with the exception of limited local lockdowns, most of the production capacity has remained open. Linglong has been able to join the procurement lists of many mid- to high-end car companies and to increase its market share. The company's 2020 net profit grew significantly to RMB 2.2 billion (USD 319 million), and its gross profit margin surpassed that of Goodyear.

Catching up with global peers

The tire industry has seen little major innovation since Michelin's pioneering radial tire design in 1946, featuring cords arranged perpendicular to the direction of travel. This technological stagnation has led to minimal qualitative differences across the global tire sector.

With the support of domestic policies, for decades, China's tire industry has invested heavily in its technological capabilities with the aim of achieving world-class standards in tire design. In 2016, Linglong unveiled China's first large-scale comprehensive tire test field in Zhaoyuan, Shandong, which is now the largest of its kind in Asia, marking China's earliest effort to establish its own product standards for tires.

By the end of the decade, China was well on the way to showing that its tires were no longer inferior to those of international brands in terms of attributes and performance. Moreover, Chinese tires came in at a cheaper cost to consumers. While being able to attract higher prices and gross profit margins, the net profit margins for international brands were generally lower than those of Chinese brands. This can be attributed to the distinct cost structure of Chinese tire companies, which significantly differs from that of international brands.

Between 2016 and 2020, market leaders such as Bridgestone and Michelin spent around 20-30% of their total costs on rubber and other raw materials and more than 30% on labor. In contrast, Chinese brands spent over 55% on raw materials and only around 10% on labor. Consequently, the market share of Chinese brands in the global tire market witnessed a substantial increase, growing from 5% in 1998 to 18% by 2019.

A winning brand strategy

As of 2020, the market size of the global tire industry was approximately USD 170 billion. Of this total, passenger vehicle tires accounted for 60% or about USD 100 billion, with an average cost of around USD 65 per unit (tire). Tires for trucks and buses accounted for around 30% of the market or about USD 50 billion, with the average cost of a single tire at around USD 226.

Linglong's brand proposition is that it provides the same quality and performance as the world's top-end manufacturers, but at better prices than its foreign competitors. The price differential charged by overseas manufacturers has more to do with their branding than any differences in the products themselves. For example, Michelin, which was established over 120 years ago, is able to extract a huge brand premium from its role as a founder in the industry, something that cannot be matched by Linglong, which is merely four decades old. While Linglong may be just as or even more competitive in terms of product development, production capacity and cost structure, it still needs to build a stronger brand in order to take on its international competition.

Domestically, Linglong launched a wide-scale effort to raise awareness and increase positive perceptions of its brand. In 2020, the company placed advertisements in elevators across 22 cities nationwide and plastered billboards in 30 airports and high-speed railway stations, exposing its brand to an estimated 300 million passengers. Moreover, the company capitalized on the massive viewership of China's national television channel, CCTV 7, by running advertisements and gaining exposure to its over 300 million viewers.

As per Figure 2, in 2020, the company spent RMB 174 million (USD 25.2 million) on advertising, equivalent to around 18% of its overall sales budget. Meanwhile, other marketing and promotional activities accounted for around RMB 35 million (USD 5.1 million) in expenses.

Figure 2   Advertising expenditure as share of total sales costs

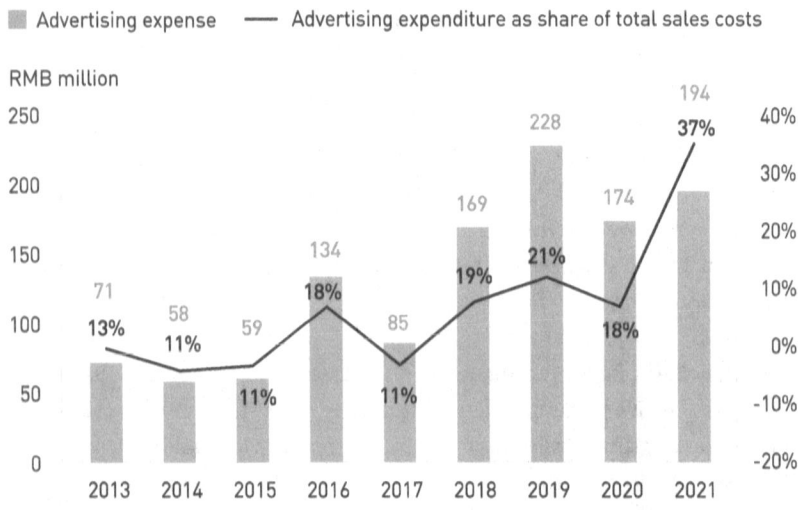

Sources: Wind Information, Topsperity Securities

Following in the footsteps of many of its international competitors, Linglong has strategically used sports advertising to bolster its brand recognition. This strategy includes sponsoring tire-related activities, such as car racing and rallies, alongside other sports like soccer and basketball. In 2018, Linglong sponsored car racing teams to rigorously test its racing tires. It also conducted product promotions in collaboration with German Bundesliga team VfL Wolfsburg and Italian Serie A team Juventus. With the NBA, Linglong became a strategic partner of Cleveland Cavaliers in 2016 and it advertised heavily during Cavalier's historic comeback against Golden State Warriors.

In China, Linglong worked with Tencent and other companies to increase investment in "new retail" strategies, while also maintaining a presence in conventional flagship stores. By 2021, there were more than 5,000 stores across China displaying the Linglong sign.

By 2021, Linglong's brand value had reached RMB 59.67 billion (USD 9.3 billion), ranking it as the 113th most valuable brand in China according to World Brand Lab and marking the 17th consecutive year that Linglong ranked among China's 500 Most Valuable Brands. According to Brand Finance, a British brand value consulting firm, Linglong was among the top 10 most valuable tire brands in the world during the two-year period from 2020 to 2021 and it has been the only Chinese tire brand on the list to date.

Figure 3   Linglong Tire's market capitalization

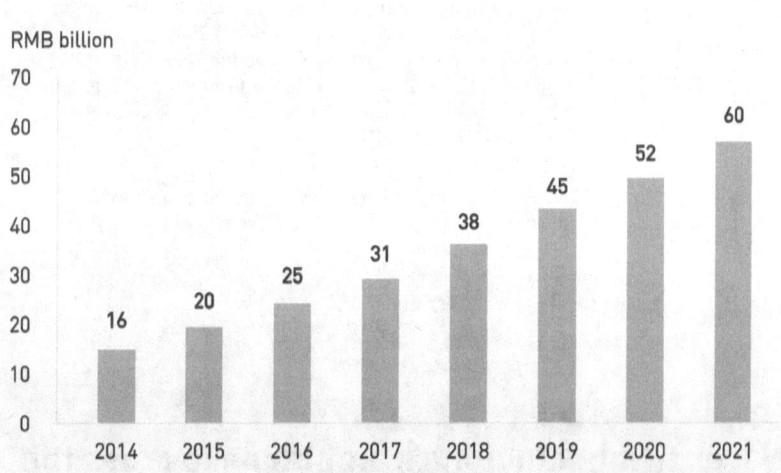

Sources: World Brand Lab, Topsperity Securities

Table 1   Linglong Tire brand portfolio

Brand name	Brand positioning
Linglong	First established in 1975, Linglong is a professional, large-scale, global and tech-driven manufacturer. Linglong products are widely used in passenger cars, commercial vehicles and construction machinery.
ATLAS	The ATLAS brand was first registered in the 1920s by American Standard. It was acquired in 1934 by the largest tire and spare parts company in the U.S., going on to become a best-selling brand. In 2009, as part of its globalization strategy, Linglong bought the ATLAS brand and relaunched it in the North American market as a new high-end tire brand in 2010. In 2017, ATLAS was officially introduced to China.
Leao	Registered in 2003, Leao is one of Linglong's newest brands, which targets a younger segment that is more fashion conscious.

Source: Topsperity Securities

Never tiring: Linglong's ambitions to cross the price threshold

Historically, global tire producers and brands have always been dependent on the fate of the car ecosystems they supply. For example, the South Korean tire company Hankook primarily supplies South Korean car factories and has expanded to serve Japanese and German car factories as well. Meanwhile, Bridgestone, a Japanese tire company, mainly supplies Japanese and American car factories.

The rise of the Chinese car industry — particularly in the electric vehicle (EV) sector — has pushed Chinese tire brands beyond the phase of "increasing market share" to "crossing the price threshold." The development of EVs has re-set the starting line for tire firms, leveling the playing field between Chinese tire producers and international first-mover brands. As a result, the barrier to entry that stems from long-established partnerships between first-mover tire brands and auto manufacturers can be bypassed. With new car manufacturers producing different types of vehicles, Chinese tires have accordingly produced tires with cost and technical advantages.

As recently as 10 years ago, Chinese OEM producers were for the most part joint ventures. Chinese tire companies struggled to gain a share of the auto parts market just on the basis of their price and quality. Since then, as domestic car brands have developed, Linglong has had a chance to catch up and even gain a firm foothold in the global market. Nowadays, it is not unusual for Linglong tires to be used in high-end automobiles, and even sometimes in the types of luxury vehicles that cost millions. Meanwhile, international tire companies that had previously been able to rely on brand barriers are losing their competitive advantages. Having tasted success, Chinese companies are now setting their sights further afield.

Interestingly, thus far there has been little crossover amongst the top 10 car models sold in the United States, Europe and China, including in terms of the tires they use. The tires used outside of China are generally larger in size and have higher specifications, generating higher profits. Being able to tap into overseas markets offers Chinese tire companies the chance to cross the price threshold. This has been boosted further by the rapid rise of China's own auto industry, and the global switch from internal combustion engine vehicles to EVs.

However, the main bottleneck for Chinese tire companies continues to be branding. Even now, international tire companies still generate ten times more revenue than Chinese ones. Hence, there is still ample opportunity for Chinese producers to step up, to extract a greater price premium and to take a greater share of the global market.

"Talent, R&D, marketing, manufacturing, branding and cooperation — these are the six aspects we must internationalize," said Wang Feng, chairman of Linglong Tire, regarding the company's strategic goals. "We should grasp this moment to extend our brand overseas. In the next three years, we want to reach three billion impressions a year." He added, "Brand building is indeed a long-term task, which takes time and is built on a company's culture and customer satisfaction. In the future, we will continue to build brand awareness and enhance brand reputation through three dimensions: products, service and value, enhancing our brand's core competitiveness."

Achieving brand breakthrough through digitalization

Digitalization has played a key role in Linglong's bid to build brand recognition and preference. In fact, since 2017, Linglong has been planning its new retail strategy, and in 2019 announced its "digital transformation" plan after signing an agreement with Tencent, the entertainment and technology conglomerate, and HUAZHI IMT, a global intelligent manufacturing solution provider and system integrator. Linglong's digitalization efforts were subsequently accelerated due to the COVID-19 pandemic.

Traditionally, the tire business has taken a simple approach: manufacturers produced tires and sold them to dealers. But with changing consumer demands, new market trends and growing domestic car sales, Linglong needed a new way to improve consumer awareness and loyalty in the increasingly digital landscape.

The new retail approach

When COVID-19 struck, Linglong's switch to the new retail model was accelerated in order to assist dealers to quickly resume sales, even if they had not been able to be physically open for business. In April 2020, Linglong, in collaboration with Tencent and HUAZHI IMT, jointly launched a smart marketing cloud platform, which was at that point the global tire industry's first ever "industrial internet" platform.

The first step in the process was to gather available data on dealership, store and consumer activities. All activities, including factory deliveries, inventory changes in warehouses and store sales, were tracked through scans of QR codes on tires. Through combining sales and services, precision marketing and branding, the platform empowered stores and dealers and supported offline consumption.

Digitalizing the whole process helped Linglong identify data gaps, more accurately match supply with demand and integrate information between Linglong and its dealer channels, which consequently made its production and logistics more agile and intelligent.

Linglong Tire's "new retail" strategies

Goals

- Establish a global platform for industrial services
- Build a sustainable, fully-connected smart marketing service platform for Linglong Tire's customers and partners
- Optimize the service system and service processes
- Create zero-distance interactive marketing for brand consumers
- Transform the company orientation from manufacturing to services, so as to speed up industrial transformation and upgrade
- Integrate data and information across R&D, production and distribution
- Optimize dealers' efficiency
- Improve store operations and management, including customer relationship management, operational support and statistical analysis

Areas affected by digitalization

1. **Order process**: The store-dealer-manufacturer relationship shifted to a digital approach. Brick-and-mortar stores supported in-store online ordering and participated in promotional activities with loyalty points that could be redeemed for future purchases.

2. **Product circulation**: By scanning codes on its products, Linglong could register and obtain real-time market sales data. The company was able to more efficiently plan its production schedules based on sales data from its channels and information about existing inventory. The sales system also benefited from the scanning as data about consumers was collected through processes such as tire insurance sales, helping establish an invaluable database of user information.

3. **Marketing operations**: By connecting digital marketing platforms with digital store systems, Linglong empowered retail stores to better understand and interact with consumers. Store managers gained valuable insights into consumer behavior and were better equipped to tailor their marketing strategies accordingly.

Successful outcomes

The additional data that Linglong gathered has improved its overall efficiency and provided an advantage over other tire makers. Its data system has helped dealers and stores with their operational management, helping them move toward low or even zero inventory. As the system has become better known across the industry, dealers have swarmed to join.

While the first two phases of the new retail strategy have focused on digitalizing distribution channels, the subsequent phase concentrated on end users, with the aim of building brand loyalty through offering products and services that align with customer preferences.

Each year, there are approximately 10 million car owners in China who purchase Linglong tires. One of the objectives of the new retail strategy is to increase sales through replacement tires.

The improved knowledge of Linglong's customer base has fed into upstream digitalization of production lines and supply chains. With better understanding of their needs, Linglong has been able to meet consumer requirements, which brings with it increased consumer loyalty.

According to Wang, "If new retail goes well, our sales of replacement tires will double in three years. By 2025, Linglong tire users will reach at least 50 million. China has 300 million drivers, which means Linglong Tire's will occupy more than 20% of the market."

Among the multiple paths to connect with end users, Linglong cooperates with OEM producers and offers ultra-long maintenance warranties to car owners, as well as a one-click settlement service via the company's official mini-app. The range of services offered encourages consumers to log on regularly. A WeChat mini-app guides users to tens of thousands of brick-and-mortar stores across the country where they can purchase Linglong goods and services.

Digitalization has helped Linglong to connect branches and service centers with online sales and offline access, ultimately benefiting consumers.

It has been somewhat difficult for the tire sector to leverage digitalization, since transportation and installation are complex and costs are high. However, there are opportunities so long as a manufacturer has a direct connection with a consumer. For example, an order placed by a user via the Linglong app will be matched with the nearest warehouse and store, ensuring it is fulfilled as quickly and efficiently as possible.

According to Cai Yi, VP of Tencent Cloud, digitalization has helped Linglong shift from a simple manufacturer to a platform service provider and a user operator.

Further plans

Linglong has indicated its intention to bring its new retail model to serve its wide range of dealers, flagship stores, brand stores and cooperative stores throughout China.

In 2020, it announced its plans to build 300 strategic cooperative dealerships, 2,000 flagship stores, 5,000 core brand stores and 60,000 cooperative stores across the country by the end of 2023.

With more warehouses, the aim is to have a delivery schedule that can take tires from the central warehouse to more than 3,000 front warehouses or flagship stores within three hours and then on the retail stores within 30 minutes.

Digitally-empowered tire stores enable Linglong to develop what it refers to as a "smart, comprehensive marketing cloud platform for customers, products and partners to connect people to people, people to things, and things to things."

Linglong's car care stations, one-stop shops for consumers, provide a comprehensive range of services. In addition to tire-related services, they offer car maintenance and repair services, oil replacement and auto detailing.

Looking further ahead to the next ten years, Linglong has said it will work on building brand awareness. The company also plans to provide support to truck drivers by setting up an assistance channel in its WeChat mini-app, as a way of giving back to society and enhancing its brand image among potential users. Furthermore, Linglong will continue to be engaged in sports sponsorships and collaborate with sports teams to achieve greater impact. Linglong also aims to reach a younger target market through its connections in the e-sports sector. To increase exposure, Linglong will run marketing campaigns on major social media channels such as WeChat, Weibo, Douyin, Kuaishou and Huochebao, a truck hire application.

In the whole life cycle of a car, Chinese consumers only change tires 1.1 times on average, making it challenging for manufacturers of durable goods such as Linglong to build and maintain strong connections with consumers. However, Linglong's commitment to digitalization holds the promise of bridging this gap. By embracing cutting-edge technology and leveraging the power of data-driven strategies, Linglong has a unique opportunity to strengthen its brand presence and drive future growth.

Updates

- Linglong's brand value continues to increase, up by nearly RMB 15 billion (USD 2.1 billion) in 2023.

- Implementation of the new retail model continues apace, though it is not clear whether the ambitious targets outlined above will be attained. By the end of June 2023, the company had developed 243 ATLAS stores and 241 Linglong outlets.

- Linglong's next production base will be built in the Americas.

- Linglong reported a net profit of RMB 1 billion (USD 142 million) in the first three quarters of 2023, up 344% YoY.

Powering Ahead
How TCL Transformed and Upgraded

Jing Bing, Associate Professor of Marketing, Cheung Kong Graduate School of Business

Meng Fanyi, Researcher, Case Center, Cheung Kong Graduate School of Business

Li Mengjun, Senior Researcher, Case Center, Cheung Kong Graduate School of Business

At the turn of the millennium, TV manufacturers in China were still heavily reliant upon imported LCD screens and had little bargaining power against their overseas suppliers such as Samsung. At a cost of more than RMB 10,000 (USD 1,208), locally-made LCD TV sets were a luxury purchase.

However, by 2008, LCD-related products made up 4% of Chinese imports, ranking fourth among 4,500 imported goods. Over the next decade, China underwent significant innovation, and by 2017, it had outpaced South Korea to become the world's top exporter of LCD panels.

Figure 1 LCD panel imports into China

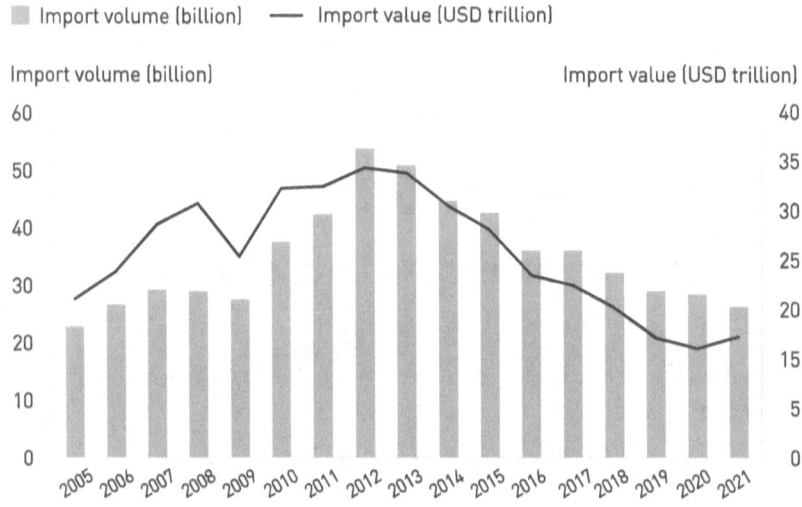

Sources: China Customs, Wind Information

This remarkable change within a decade is just one example of how China has transformed from being a simple assembler of TVs and smartphones into a manufacturer of more complicated components such as display panels and batteries. Among the many manufacturing trailblazers, TCL, which had a consolidated total revenue of more than RMB 260 billion (USD 38.7 billion) in 2022, showcases how a business can turn itself around to become a leader in its category.

From cassette tape producer to global manufacturing powerhouse

TCL's humble beginnings can be traced back to 1981 when it was established as a cassette tape producer in Huizhou, Guangdong. Its product range subsequently expanded to include telephones, stereos, color TVs, mobile phones, air conditioners, refrigerators and washing machines. By 2002, TCL was one of China's leading domestic consumer electronics manufacturers.

In 2004, TCL set its sights on the global market. It acquired Thomson's TV business and formed a joint venture, with TCL holding a controlling stake of 67%. However, soon after this acquisition, the industry witnessed a seismic shift as cutting-edge LCD and plasma displays superseded the older cathode ray tube (CRT) technology. This abrupt change rendered TCL's recent acquisition obsolete, transforming it from a source of television-related expertise that could facilitate TCL's global expansion into a financial challenge. This merges and acquisitions (M&A) experience underscored for Li Dongsheng, the founder and chairman of TCL, the critical importance of possessing the most up-to-date technology in positioning a business in the value chain.

However, to upgrade from manufacturing to R&D of LCD panels required significant investment and strong market demand. If the panels produced could not be sold to generate cash flow for the company, the investment would have failed or even backfired. Having seen that LCD TVs comprised 67% of the overall TV market share in mainland China in 2008, with a 51% YoY increase, TCL felt certain that its 2007 partnership with Samsung to jointly invest in a liquid crystal module factory had been a smart move, providing TCL with invaluable insights into the LCD industry.

The 2008 financial crisis hit demand hard. The LCD display industry, like many others, experienced a decline. However, compared with the West, China's economy for the most part withstood the financial headwinds and soon entered a recovery phase. Li saw the crisis as providing an opportunity for Chinese enterprises to upgrade. By then, TVs were still a key contributor of revenue for TCL, even while LCD technology was prevailing over CRT displays. Chinese TV manufacturers were heavily reliant upon imported components, lagging behind in technology and seeing thinning profit margins.

Li once again recognized the significance of obtaining a technological advantage. He observed how South Korean panel firms, albeit entering the market later, had strategically invested in upstream R&D initiatives and emerged victorious against their Japanese rivals during the 1990s.

He believed that mainland China would follow on from South Korea to become the next hub for the display panel industry, driven in large part by robust domestic demand.

Additionally, he anticipated that TCL could leverage its TV manufacturing capacity and robust sales force to benefit from the vertical integration of display panel and TV production. In 2010, the successful sale of 13 million TCL television sets worldwide confirmed that its investment in LCD technology had indeed been a wise decision.

Screen time: building the foundations for success at TCL CSOT

In November 2009, TCL deepened its involvement in the market with the establishment in Shenzhen of China Star Optoelectronics Technology (TCL CSOT), a company manufacturing display panels.

To lay the foundation for success for TCL CSOT, TCL needed to ensure it had adequate resources and talent. To this end, TCL recruited an elite squad of engineers, technicians and managers from Taiwan, South Korea and Japan, bringing together an international team that already had technical capabilities and industry experience, helping TCL CSOT to quickly gain an initial foothold in the industry.

Investment in TCL CSOT came from internal funding with the backing of TCL, the Shenzhen government and a bank consortium. The initial investment in its first production line was RMB 24.5 billion (USD 3.6 billion), equivalent to more than 50 times TCL's net profit that year.

Over the next decade, TCL CSOT successively built multiple production bases in locations including Wuhan, Huizhou and Guangzhou in China, and Andhra Pradesh in southern India. The company also acquired a Samsung factory in Suzhou. In 2021, TCL CSOT's operating revenue was RMB 88 billion (USD 13.6 billion), and its net profit was more than RMB 10 billion (USD 1.6 billion). As of 2022, TCL CSOT had nine panel production lines and five module bases, at a total investment of more than RMB 260 billion (USD 38.7 billion).

With ongoing investment, TCL CSOT continues to dominate the global LCD display panel industry.

Prioritizing efficiency

Efficiency must be prioritized by any latecomer entering a high-tech, capital-intensive industry with long-term returns. This was the case with TCL CSOT, which initially achieved cost leadership by producing lower-tier products with mature technology. Subsequently, it progressively transitioned toward developing differentiated products and technologies, and reinvested profits in technological advancements.

In fact, TCL CSOT has consistently improved its production efficiency through various strategies. First, it adopted advanced technologies to enhance its production capacity, resulting in a significant increase in gross margins. Second, the company maximized equipment utilization by focusing on manufacturing mainstream products for key customers. Third, TCL CSOT significantly shortened production ramp-up times, allowing for quicker turnaround and improved product yield. Fourth, it has optimized its production line layout, as well as its product offerings to adapt to its customer portfolio. Through operational efficiency, TCL CSOT effectively generates revenue that can be subsequently reinvested in both capacity expansion and research and development.

Developing core products and technologies

Having gained a secure foothold in the industry, TCL CSOT turned its focus to developing advanced products and technologies. The company adopted a strategic product strategy, commencing with the introduction of products with straightforward technical specifications and affordable price points.

As TCL CSOT gained momentum, it gradually shifted its focus to developing high-end products. In terms of its product portfolio, TCL

CSOT initially concentrated on making significant advancements within individual product categories, ensuring that each offering met the highest standards of quality. Subsequently, the company expanded its scope to encompass a broader range of products to meet the demands of the market.

Figure 2 TCL CSOT product portfolio

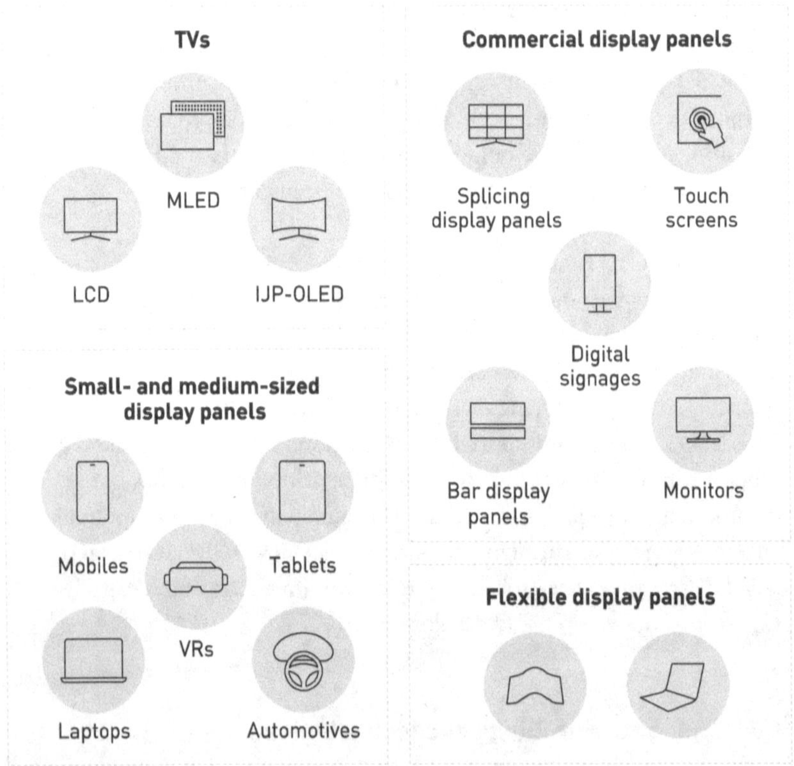

TVs: LCD, MLED, IJP-OLED

Small- and medium-sized display panels: Mobiles, Tablets, VRs, Laptops, Automotives

Commercial display panels: Splicing display panels, Touch screens, Digital signages, Bar display panels, Monitors

Flexible display panels

Source: TCL CSOT

In 2022, TCL CSOT achieved the second-highest global ranking in terms of TV panel shipments. The company ranked first worldwide in shipments of interactive whiteboard panels, e-sports panels and low-temperature polycrystalline silicon (LTPS) tablet panels, second for LTPS laptop panels, and third globally for LTPS mobile phone panels. Automotive-related panels are becoming an increasingly important product category.

TCL CSOT has spearheaded new display technologies such as Mini LED, printed OLED, QLED and Micro-LED through a combination of R&D and partnerships. In 2021, TCL CSOT publicly registered 1,954 international patents under the International Patent System, ranking eighth globally in terms of total numbers of patents and fourth among Chinese companies. As of 2022, it had the world's second highest number of patent applications for electroluminescence quantum dot technology and materials.

Feeding the ecosystem

To be an industry leader requires engagement in all aspects of that industry's ecosystem. The manufacturing process of panels involves the utilization of more than one hundred raw materials, which requires seamless collaboration throughout the supply chain and management of key industry stakeholders.

According to Yan Xiaolin, head of the TCL Industrial Research Institute, the next-generation display technology will likely come about through the development of innovative materials. To this end, TCL has formed strategic partnerships with top-tier upstream players including DuPont and Corning from the U.S. and Sumitomo Chemical and Nissan Chemical from Japan. Cooperation with a variety of players at different points in the value chain has helped TCL successfully develop various new display prototypes. In 2020, TCL CSOT established a joint laboratory with Sanan Semiconductor to develop micro-LED display technology.

By engaging with partners, investing in research and development, and strategically aligning resources, TCL CSOT has effectively cultivated a thriving ecosystem that enables it to remain at the forefront of technological advancements in the industry.

Solar activity: the emergence of TCL Zhonghuan

The experience of success in panels boosted TCL's confidence to expand into other technological areas. In 2017, TCL laid out its plans to venture into industries with a focus on capital-intensive sectors relying on new and emerging technology. Since then, the company has organized its operations in accordance with this strategic direction.

In 2019, TCL Group experienced a major asset restructuring and split into two entities: TCL Technology and TCL Industries. TCL Technology is comprised of TCL CSOT and other entities related to semiconductor display, while TCL Industries mainly includes businesses producing TVs and white goods.

In 2020, TCL announced its vision to become a world-leading intelligent technology industry group. It made the decision to move into the solar photovoltaic industry, having considered the structure of the industry, the potential demand and TCL's own capabilities. That year, TCL Technology acquired the Tianjin Zhonghuan Electronic Information Group.

Following the acquisition, TCL Zhonghuan, formerly known as Tianjin Zhonghuan Semiconductor Co., Ltd, a subsidiary of Tianjin Zhonghuan Electronic Information Group, underwent a significant transformation. It has since kept a leading role in the field of new energy photovoltaics, focusing on essential products crucial to solar panel technology. These products include photovoltaic silicon wafers, photovoltaic cells, photovoltaic components. It is also involved in the development of photovoltaic power stations. Semiconductor displays and photovoltaics exhibit many similarities in terms of operational management and technology, which explains why TCL has chosen to operate across both industries.

By 2022, TCL Zhonghuan's operating revenue reached RMB 67 billion (USD 10 billion), a YoY increase of 63%. Net profit was RMB 6.82 billion (USD 1 billion), a YoY increase of 69%. TCL Zhonghuan has become the new growth engine for TCL. With an anticipated boom in the green energy sector, the future looks bright for the company.

Figure 3 Financial performance of TCL Zhonghuan

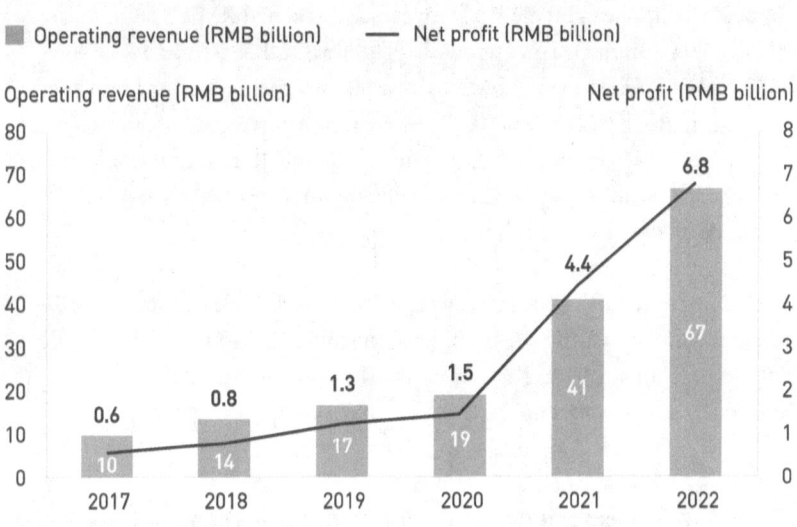

Source: Wind Information

Expanding advanced capacity

Li has been quoted as saying, "If you want to stay ahead, you must lead in quantity and scale." In the past two years, TCL Zhonghuan has actively expanded production around its top-performing products. In February 2021, it launched its 12th generation (G12) large-size silicon wafer project, with an investment of RMB 12.7 billion (USD 2 billion). Production started in Ningxia, China, in January 2022. Currently, TCL Zhonghuan holds the largest market share globally in the G12 silicon wafer market. By the end of 2022, the company's annual production capacity of monocrystalline silicon wafers for photovoltaics had reached 140 GW, an increase of 150% over the previous two years. Contributing around 90% of the 140 GW, the G12 project with its strong capacity propelled TCL Zhonghuan to be the world's foremost monocrystalline silicon wafer manufacturer.

Reducing costs and improving efficiency

In 2021, TCL Zhonghuan's R&D investment reached RMB 2.58 billion (USD 399.9 million), a YoY increase of 183%. Of this, RMB 1.97 billion (USD 305.4 million) went toward research into cost reduction, with the remaining RMB 610 million (USD 94.6 million) invested in technological innovation. As a result, TCL Zhonghuan was able to reduce its consumption of silicon by nearly 3% per unit of product and increase the monthly production of silicon rods by 30%.

It also upgraded its smart factory capabilities and levels of automation, dramatically increasing the number of machines that one operator could attend to from 4 to 384. This has elevated the single-line production efficiency to levels that are 50% higher than those of competitors.

Transferring experience and core competitiveness

TCL Zhonghuan and TCL CSOT display many similarities, especially in terms of industrial strategic setup, risk management and operational styles. At the supply chain level, the two also share many of the same suppliers. In terms of resources, TCL Zhonghuan has been able to leverage TCL CSOT's wealth of talent, technology and capital. In 2021, with an optimized debt structure and reduced financial costs, TCL Zhonghuan reduced its financial expenses YoY by 18%.

Looking to the future, TCL Zhonghuan can also learn from TCL CSOT's rich experience in industrial chain integration and industrial investment. Moreover, TCL Zhonghuan's global expansion plans will likely benefit from having access to the TCL manufacturing and sales systems that are already well-established throughout Europe, North America, South America and India. At the same time, developments at TCL Zhonghuan have supported perceptions of TCL overall and have helped strengthen its semiconductor display business.

Figure 4 Financial performance of TCL Technology

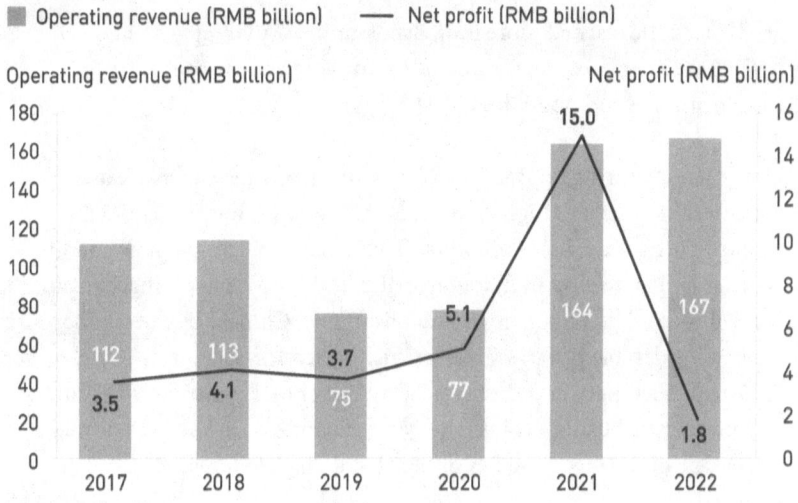

Source: Wind Information

The establishment of TCL CSOT has been a crucial step in the transformation and upgrading of TCL. Through mastering several key links in the industrial supply chain, TCL has grown its downstream business and built invaluable production and management capabilities in the high-tech sector, which it has been able to leverage as it has developed into a globally-leading, large-scale, high-tech industrial group.

Moving into solar energy, TCL has found success in aligning its strategic development goals with China's broader industrial policies.

Over the past decade, TCL has transformed itself from a traditional consumer electronics manufacturer into a large-scale, high-tech industrial group with three core industries: smart terminals, semiconductor displays and photovoltaic solar energy.

Navigating upstream and downstream

So what can be learned more broadly about the overall upgrading of Chinese manufacturing from our examination of the specific transformation and upgrading of TCL?

First, manufacturing upgrading involves upstream and downstream activities. In upstream high-tech fields, China has achieved significant results in areas such as supercomputers, satellite navigation, new energy vehicles and large aircraft manufacturing. Driven by market mechanisms and without relying upon government support, Chinese businesses have made considerable progress in areas such as semiconductor displays, electrical machinery and mechanical equipment. The entry of TCL and other domestic businesses into the panel manufacturing sector has made China one of the main engines of the global display industry.

In tandem with the development of the upstream industrial chain, there is a crucial need to establish influential global brands and set industry standards downstream. In this respect, Chinese home appliance companies have played a pioneering role. For instance, TCL has steadily expanded its market share of smart screens on the international stage, consistently ranking among the top three global manufacturers for many years. TCL has worked to build awareness and positive perceptions of the brand through various means, including sponsorship of top international events, such as the FIBA EuroBasket 2022.

Looking to the future, it is imperative to emphasize the development of international standards for both products and technology. This could help TCL establish a brand position as a technological forerunner and also support the development of a recognizable, well-regarded brand.

Second, technological and managerial innovation can both play roles in business development. Technological innovation has been a vital driving force for the upgrading of Chinese industry. While the country has made some breakthroughs in certain core technologies, China still often lags behind developed economies in both hardware and software. TCL and the development of the Chinese semiconductor display industry have shown that critical technologies cannot just be procured. Cultivating and attracting innovative talent, and in particular bringing together leading international talent with the necessary technical and industrial experience, can help a country grow toward being self-reliant in high-tech areas.

Innovative management also plays a role in industrial upgrading. The rise of manufacturing in the U.S. and Japan has been based not only on technological progress, but also on the development of business management expertise. For companies, technological advancement usually plateaus after reaching a certain level. It is at this time that innovative management may stimulate further growth opportunities.

Third, a business can be a jack of all trades or master of one. Enterprises that have already excelled in the key links of the industrial chain can choose to continue to explore along the original industrial chain or expand into new industries. TCL, for instance, from the outset specialized in semiconductor displays but later diversified by entering the photovoltaic industry through the acquisition of Zhonghuan, thereby establishing itself as a global high-tech player.

Fourth, it is always important to empower the supply chain. The high-tech industry tends to be highly integrated, involving many stakeholders. As a result, enterprises may find it difficult to upgrade when its upstream and downstream supply chain players lag behind. TCL has championed collaborative innovation. With more companies like TCL, the entire industrial chain will strengthen.

Recent shifts in geopolitics have added complexity to international trade dynamics, underlining the significance of constructing robust global industrial chains. The export of Chinese industrial manufacturing capabilities, beyond just products, is likely to emerge as a significant trend. Pioneering companies such as TCL are at the forefront of this evolution, forging new pathways and contributing to the evolution of global industrial chains.

Updates

- TCL CSOT is constantly developing new products. As of the end of 2022, TCL CSOT had a total of 58,942 global patent applications and 22,385 global patent authorizations.

- Efforts to build positive brand perceptions continue, with TCL being named the Official Partner of the American NFL, a sponsor of the Spanish and Italian national football teams, and a sponsor of the Copa Libertadores de América football league.

- During 2023, TCL Zhonghuan expanded further downstream in the photovoltaic industry by building a high-efficiency solar battery factory. Its revenue climbed to RMB 34.9 billion (USD 5 million) in the first half of 2023, with profits up 50% over the same period.

- TCL Technology reported that net profits in the first half of 2023 had increased by 24%.

Chapter Three

Chinese Brands Meeting the Needs of Global Tastes

Many Chinese brands have experienced remarkable growth in expanding their presence globally, using their innovative business models to cater to the diverse preferences of international consumers. With China's domestic market becoming increasingly saturated, companies such as SHEIN and Yili have ventured abroad, focusing on markets with substantial spending power. This section explores how these exceptional Chinese brands have effectively penetrated international markets.

Case Studies

7 Need for Speed
How SHEIN Became a Global Online Fashion Retailer

8 The Cream of the Crop
Yili's Ambitions to Build a Global Dairy Company

Need for Speed

How SHEIN Became a Global Online Fashion Retailer

Zhu Yang, Professor of Operations Management, Cheung Kong Graduate School of Business

Wang Xiaolong, Senior Researcher, Case Center, Cheung Kong Graduate School of Business

SHEIN's "real-time fashion" model has redefined the fast fashion business. Its approach to producing clothes and selling them through its cross-border e-commerce platform has provided a new benchmark for manufacturers and brands in the internet era.

SHEIN's development trajectory, market positioning and values have greatly diverged from other more conventional export-oriented cross-border e-commerce companies in China. Over the past ten years, SHEIN has built up its capabilities to generate demand and provide supply using a highly advanced digitalization system and leveraged its value proposition to develop cross-border markets.

Due to these strategic efforts, during just one single month — May 2021 — the SHEIN app was downloaded more than 14 million times. In May 2022, it held the top position across all categories in the U.S. iPhone App Store, surpassing giants such as TikTok, Instagram and Twitter and Amazon. In 2022, SHEIN entered the top ten of the Kantar BrandZ™

Chinese Global Brands listing.

According to Leadleo, an independent industry research organization, SHEIN's total revenue in 2020 was approximately RMB 70 billion (USD 10 billion), and it enjoyed an astounding compound annual growth rate of 189% between 2015 and 2020. Following Series E funding in 2020, the firm was valued at more than USD 15 billion.

SHEIN's market entry

The gloves are off: the early days of cross-border e-commerce

Similar to domestic e-commerce in China, the cross-border e-commerce business among Chinese companies has been shaped by fierce competition. A large number of cross-border e-commerce companies has established online stores, some through Amazon and some through their own websites. They have used various search engine optimization tactics to attract global traffic, analyzing data from tools such as Google Analytics to maximize sales.

However, particularly in the early days of e-commerce, when there was only minimal consumer protection, online customers ran the risk of falling prey to unscrupulous vendors, some of whom engaged in deceitful practices such as sending empty packages, falsely claiming bankruptcy after receiving payment, selling counterfeit or inferior products, using non-copyrighted images and delivering products that did not match their descriptions.

These challenges were compounded in cross-border transactions, due to issues such as information asymmetry, minimal regulations and cultural differences. With no concern for their longer-term reputation, some vendors set out to make quick money, sometimes on one-shot deals.

SHEIN's singular style choices: taking a long-term approach

In a marketplace plagued with ethical concerns, it appears all too easy to take the fastest route to success. However, any business with long-term goals is advised to adopt the principled approach. From the outset, SHEIN's founder Xu Yangtian and his team deliberately took a different path from other vendors who were chasing the fast buck, instead making strategic decisions that would go on to form the basis for the company's future long-term success.

With a background in traffic-driven business, Xu set up his first cross-border e-commerce venture in 2009, selling wedding dresses in an approach that was similar to the market leader at the time, LightInTheBox. In 2012, Xu pivoted from wedding dresses to establish a more comprehensive cross-border clothing business for women, SheInside, the forerunner of SHEIN. In early media coverage, Xu is quoted as having explained that "to build a brand, you must find professional people and operate it professionally. The business model of selling cheap products at a markup is not sustainable."

SHEIN rarely participates in media interviews, releases press statements only sparingly and is not yet publicly listed. An analysis of the company's activities and performance has shown that it is SHEIN's marketing initiatives, efficient supply chain, extensive product offerings, and digital technologies that have enabled SHEIN to outperform competitors.

As shown in Figure 1 on the following page, SHEIN has established its own processes and has made various deliberate decisions about how it should operate, which is in stark contrast to the sometimes less systematic approach of its competitors, many of whom have been purely focused on growing their sales.

Figure 1 SHEIN's operational processes

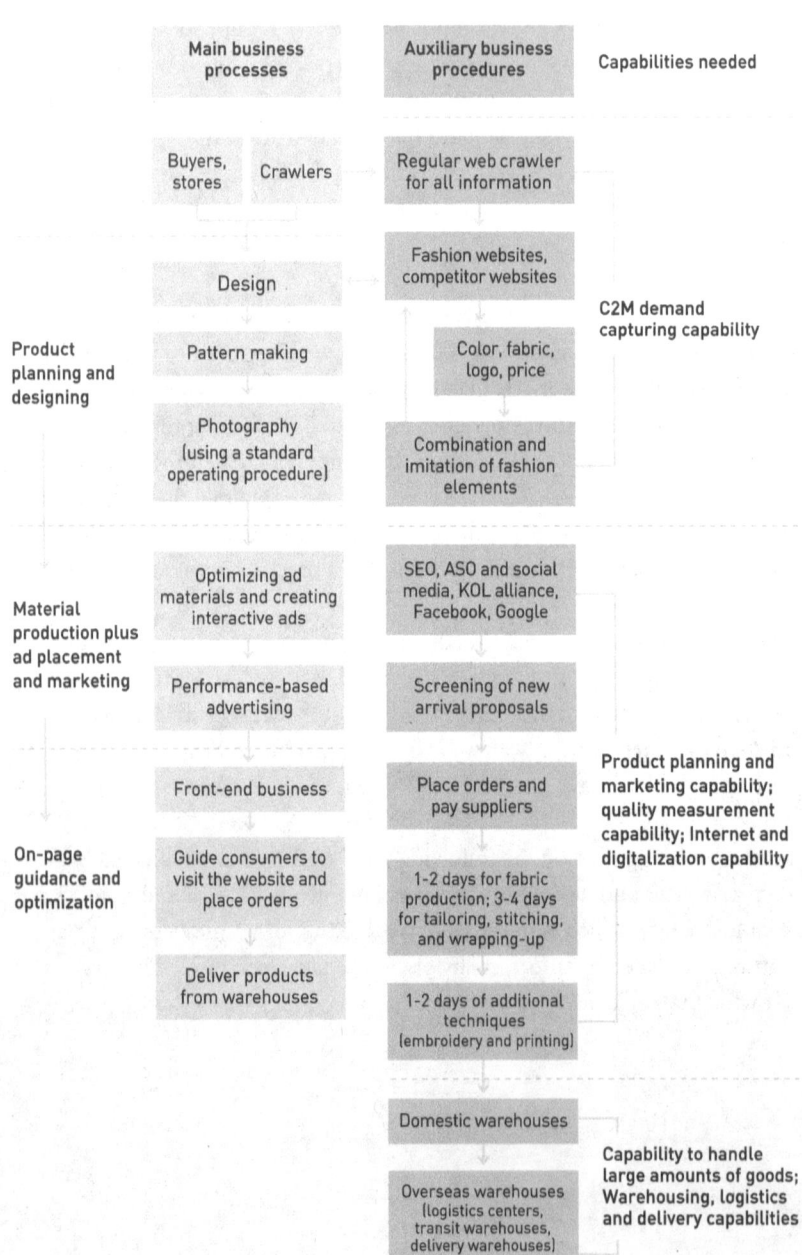

Source: Zheshang Securities

Satisfying the demand

Fashion forward: the global e-commerce market and consumer characteristics

Globally, the retail industry has witnessed a shift toward online channels in recent years. The penetration of e-commerce in the United States increased from 6% in 2010 to 21% in 2020. Chinese brands have grown in popularity due to improvements in quality while maintaining affordability. From 2017 to 2020, the proportion of Chinese stores on Amazon rose from 23% to 42%.

In China, Alibaba, JD.com and Pinduoduo dominated the e-commerce market in 2020, collectively commanding 84% of the market share. Outside of China, however, concentration rates of e-commerce tend to be far lower. For instance, even the top 10 e-commerce companies in the U.K. accounted for only 68% of the total market in 2019. Similarly, the top 10 players in the U.S. made up just 63% of the market that year.

In 2022, clothing, shoes and bags accounted for 33% of cross-border e-commerce from China. This burgeoning sector is primarily focused on consumers aged 18-35. In 2020, 56% of global cross-border e-commerce consumers were millennials and Gen-Z. That year, 22% of millennials and 17% of Gen-Z spent more than USD 500 on cross-border e-commerce.

Dressed for the occasion: SHEIN's demand-side digital marketing strategy

Generating online traffic is a key factor of success for any online marketer. To be effective, businesses must maximize their traffic, whether attracting instant attention with quick, short-term rewards, or gaining longer-term traffic built on trustworthy brands that add value over time.

One of the key marketing tactics used by SHEIN has been to leverage the traffic of global social media platforms, such as Facebook, Twitter, Instagram and YouTube, amassing tens of millions of dedicated followers. The company excels in social media advertising, curating high-quality posts that resonate with its core customer base. Around 90% of SHEIN's posts are images centered around themes such as women, pets and picturesque settings.

In addition, SHEIN understands the significance of localization. It has registered distinct accounts in different countries with content presented in local languages, thereby establishing a direct and relatable brand that directly connects with local audiences.

Traffic data shows that more people come to the website having searched for the keyword 'SHEIN' than via paid search links, and that the proportion coming through keyword searches is increasing. From the proportion of users making a direct beeline to its homepage, it can be inferred that SHEIN has built up a solid, well-known and reliable brand.

SHEIN has attracted low-cost traffic using global social media and has established a huge user-generated content (UGC) marketing network. Rather than advertising products on Google and Facebook, SHEIN directs potential customers to its website and encourages them to download the app. While this approach may have shown less immediate effectiveness in boosting sales and has resulted in a cost-per-thousand-impressions (CPM) that has been around 50% higher than its competitors, in the long term, it has helped build better consumer understanding of the SHEIN brand.

Table 1 highlights some of the distinctive features of SHEIN's marketing efforts.

Table 1   Features of SHEIN's marketing activities

Features	Description
When SHEIN was first launched, key opinion consumer (KOC) and key opinion leader (KOL) marketing was ubiquitous. Sometimes, brands did not even need to pay these influencers to promote their products.	SHEIN worked with internet celebrities to promote its products. Using this approach to generate traffic helped SHEIN keep its advertising costs down in its early days.
SHEIN encouraged its customers to share their experiences, leveraging their influence to drive product development and expansion.	SHEIN attached great importance to "user engagement." It encouraged customers to share photos of their products on Facebook photo walls, offering coupons as a reward. This helped transform SHEIN into a hub for fashion content sharing. User-generated posts also made it possible for SHEIN to identify fashion trends and develop new products.
SHEIN strategically chose dresses as a focal point for their apparel line as it was comparatively easy to develop new items within this product category.	Since its launch, SHEIN has consistently released a large number of new items - around 3,000 per week in its early days. The company initially focused on dresses as a key product category, using creative prints to differentiate styles and to increase the range of product offerings.
Even when it launched new products at a rapid pace, SHEIN showcased each product with high-quality promotional images.	SHEIN faced a lot of competition in its early days. Most of its competitors at the time were using product images sourced externally. SHEIN was resolute about using its own in-house models and producing its own cover images. This resulted in more visually appealing images and helped SHEIN obtain higher click-through and conversion rates.
Global consumers were willing to tolerate a relatively slow delivery from SHEIN.	SHEIN's initial speed of delivery was far slower than it is today. In the early days of overseas e-commerce, it was not unusual for consumers to have to wait 10 to 20 days to receive their goods. SHEIN had the breathing space to improve its operations and ultimately reduce delivery time.

Source: Zheshang Securities

Quick turnarounds and smart pricing

Fast fashion is characterized by its ability to popularize niche fashion trends and increase consumer consumption through quick access to new styles. Thus, it typically features a wide range of styles, quick product launches and low prices. These characteristics align well with SHEIN's domestic supply chain and its capacity to produce low-cost products with quick turnarounds. The significant purchasing power of millennial and Gen-Z consumers has further accelerated the growth of the fast fashion industry.

To grasp SHEIN's marketing strategies and customer targeting, it is essential to understand its products and its pricing system. SHEIN initially started selling just women's clothing, but soon expanded into 18 major product categories, including men's and children's clothing, home textiles and makeup.

SHEIN has demonstrated a clear, competitive edge in terms of both pricing and the frequency of new product releases when compared to other prominent fast fashion platforms. As shown in Table 2, in the U.S. market, the most affordable women's clothing items on SHEIN are priced at USD $10 or lower, well below the price floors set by its main competitors, ZARA and H&M.

In addition, SHEIN surpasses global fast fashion leaders in the availability of styles and designs. With tens of thousands of items available for sale at any given time, SHEIN ensures it can cater to the individual needs of an extensive consumer base.

Table 2 Price range and number of products on offer at four major fashion brands, May 2021

Women's clothing category			T-Shirts	Dresses	Jeans	Coats
SHEIN	Price (USD)	Min.	2	3	10	6
		Max.	30	95	45	130
	Products available		14,671	21,731	2,256	1,990
ZAFUL	Price (USD)	Min.	5	6	10	9
		Max.	25	46	39	72
	Products available		600	1,094	85	619
ZARA	Price (USD)	Min.	8	13	20	36
		Max.	50	149	50	90
	Products available		234	1,133	371	753
H&M	Price (USD)	Min.	5	13	10	18
		Max.	50	349	70	299
	Products available		182	582	265	294

Sources: SHEIN, ZAFUL, H&M, Zhongtai Securities

As shown in Figure 2, SHEIN can transform a design sketch into a saleable product within three weeks, with delivery to consumers in a mere four weeks. This places SHEIN's supply timeline on par with fast fashion leader ZARA's 25 days from concept to consumer – far faster than the average six-month process employed by most large-scale clothing enterprises.

Need for Speed: How SHEIN Became a Global Online Fashion Retailer

Figure 2   ZARA and SHEIN supply timelines

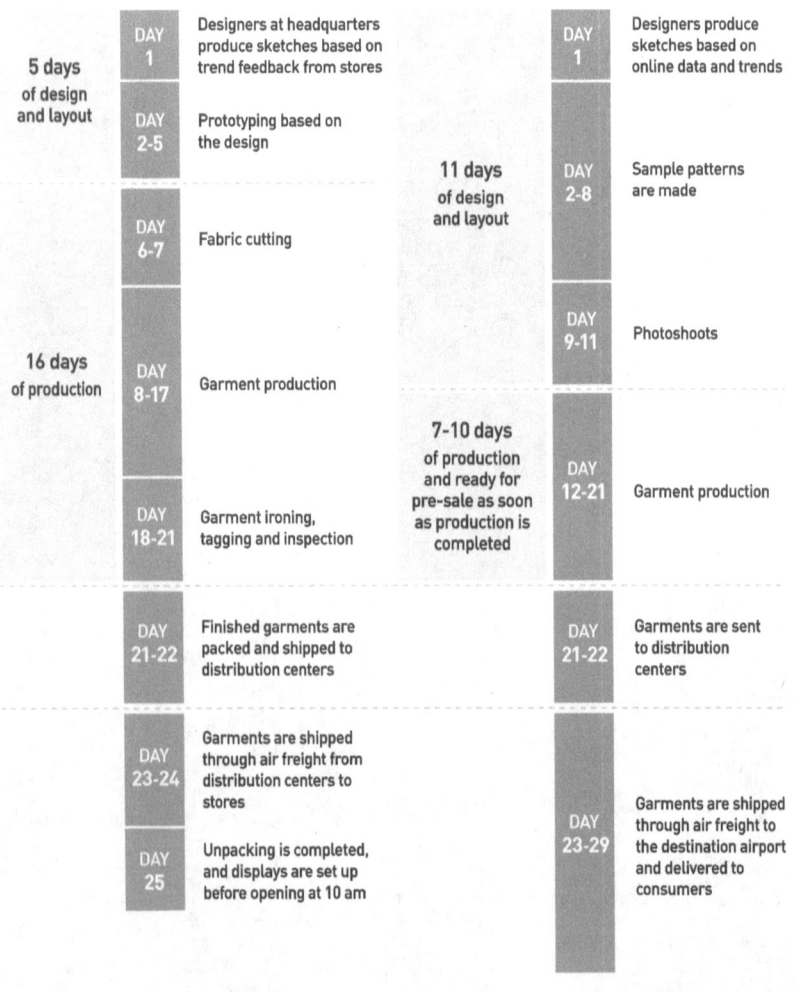

Sources: The Wall Street Journal, Zhongtai Securities

To achieve such impressive efficiency, SHEIN employs a data-driven approach to inventory management. It follows a "small-batch on-demand business model," where the company initially produces a small batch of products to test the waters, and based on performance, quickly places reorders for popular products. This is an approach that has helped to maximize sales and profits and to significantly reduce inventory.

A stitch in time: the digital supply chain

SHEIN's ability to manage its entire industrial chain and make data-driven decisions has been a major factor in its success, differentiating it from many of its competitors.

The consumer-to-manufacturer (C2M) business model and flexible supply chains have emerged as key features underpinning the development of smart manufacturing. Building a flexible supply chain can be approached in various ways. One method involves constructing a new supply chain and using advanced technologies such as artificial intelligence, robotics, big data, the Internet of Things and sophisticated manufacturing execution software. This approach allows for the integration of data-driven instructions into the production processes in a new factory or production line.

Another way is to transform an existing supply chain, particularly one characterized by numerous small workshops and factories without the financial capabilities to build automated production lines. While they may lack technological prowess, these small entities tend to be well attuned to their customers' requirements due to their long-standing relationships. Using this approach, an upgraded supply chain can be developed by an aggregator that uses its own capabilities to unite such small entities.

The media generally agrees that SHEIN is proving the feasibility of the second approach, at least in the field of fast fashion. Taking advantage of some of the fundamental advantages of China's sound supply chain, SHEIN has been able to quickly provide new products from diverse product categories at relatively low prices based on the efficiency of its supply chain. Indeed, the long-term strategy of the company appears to be based more upon having an efficient digital supply chain than building brand awareness and managing internet traffic.

In 2014, SHEIN moved its production capacity to Panyu, Guangdong, and established a logistics center in Foshan, also in Guangdong. At present, all key components of SHEIN's supply chain — design, pattern making, production and warehousing — are located in Guangdong. When recruiting new suppliers, SHEIN tends to prioritize factories based in the Pearl River Delta region. This concentration of resources in a single region has resulted in quicker delivery, reduced operating costs and improved efficiency.

Generally speaking, access to raw materials is one of the most critical factors in production cycles. To ensure that the production of popular products is not affected when being reordered, SHEIN has proactively built its own exclusive online B2B supplier platform, "Taoliaowang.com." This platform allows SHEIN to source from manufacturing and trade suppliers with sufficient inventory, which ensures that the company is able to respond quickly to market demands. As of February 2020, Taoliaowang.com reportedly had more than 300 suppliers.

Supported by its stable supply chain, each year SHEIN has been able to purchase more than 1.6 billion meters of fabric, worth more than RMB 5 billion (USD 743 million). Its numerous fabric suppliers enable the company to offer a diverse range of products. In fact, SHEIN introduces approximately 3,000 new items daily, putting it in a different league from a stark contrast to ZARA's average of two updates per week.

Looking good: analyzing the SHEIN supply chain

Despite the lack of detailed information about SHEIN's supply chain, it appears that the company has developed a robust digital system that effectively connects designers, fabric suppliers, factories, warehouses, logistics and customers.

Research into the information available has shown the challenges faced at each stage of SHEIN's supply chain, how the company addresses these challenges and why overcoming them is crucial to SHEIN's success.

SHEIN's supply chain

Stage 1   Materials

What   Developing the materials used in production requires a high degree of standardization and investment in R&D.

How   SHEIN is not directly involved in the manufacturing of the fabrics used in its products. Instead, the company prefers to cooperate with fabric manufacturers. As noted, it has built its own B2B supplier platform, Taoliaowang.com, to ensure reliability and consistency of supply.

Why   In SHEIN's product offerings, design and delivery are more important than the fabrics used. It has made the decision to allocate its resources to the areas of greatest need, rather than attempting to do everything by itself.

Stage 2   Design

What   Design is difficult to standardize, meaning limited opportunities to achieve economies of scale and to guarantee a quick response. Designer teams are often difficult to manage.

How   SHEIN uses information technology to facilitate the design process, leveraging tools including Google Trends and web crawler tools to monitor fashion trends. The design workflow has been standardized. Designers work within a designated scope, using a predetermined range of fabrics, patterns and accessories via a SaaS platform.

Why   SHEIN does not aspire to be a high-end luxury brand. Consequently, it is not vital that every design should be unique. In order to be sufficiently responsive to keep up with ever-changing trends, SHEIN trades some of its creativity for efficiency.

Stage 3	Production
What	Production is mostly handled by small workshops across China, providing a level of flexibility. However, these types of small-scale businesses may lack financial security, making them vulnerable to business failure, which would hamper SHEIN's production stability. Due to its "small batch on demand" model, SHEIN faces considerable management challenges and high transaction costs due to its numerous small-sized suppliers.
How	SHEIN's policy has been to refrain from exploiting its suppliers. In fact, the company has a deliberately short payment schedule, and even provides short-term financial assistance to suppliers if necessary. The stability of orders and cash flow helps these small-scale suppliers survive market fluctuations and enter into mutually-beneficial long-term partnerships with SHEIN. In order to maximize efficiency in managing its suppliers and minimize transaction costs, SHEIN has moved its headquarters close to where most of its suppliers are based, in Guangzhou. It has also supported its suppliers to realize the benefits of introducing — albeit somewhat rudimentary — digitalization, into their production processes.
Why	Outsourcing is cost-efficient but hard to manage. In-house production may be easy to manage but is costly. SHEIN's strategy — to be deeply involved with but to not fully control the production process — is an attempt to realize the advantages of each of these two types of approaches.

Stage 4	Warehousing and logistics
What	Overseas warehousing provides the facility to store inventory and accept returned goods. The latter is particularly important given that the return rate for fast fashion can run between 20% to 25%.

How SHEIN waives the freight charge on orders of USD 49 or more and allows customers to return goods without charge within 30 days. The generous return policy encourages customers to make bigger purchases, increasing the average transaction value. SHEIN disinfects and re-packs returned goods in its overseas warehouses, making them ready for sale again.

Why Benefiting from the tax exemptions and preferential treatment by the UPU terminal dues, SHEIN's delivery costs come in at below 20% of product prices. This enables the company to maintain its affordable pricing strategy. The overseas warehouses allow SHEIN to accept and redistribute returns. The lenient return policies increase SHEIN's average transaction value, which in turn enables SHEIN to keep logistics costs to a minimum.

Strike a pose: profitability with adaptability

Most fashion businesses operate by anticipating consumer needs and finding the common ground between product development and market demand. By contrast, fast-fashion businesses such as SHEIN and ZARA take a less targeted approach, instead aiming to cover all possible trends with their product ranges.

The fast fashion industry's model can be represented by a triangle, as illustrated in Figure 3 on the following page. In this visualization of the industry's workings, the top angle represents the large quantity of new products that are provided at a low cost, the bottom left angle shows a high price-performance ratio, and the bottom right angle shows high turnover with low inventory. Attaining profitability at a high level of investment and low gross margins requires a highly efficient approach, one in which inventory is kept to a minimum.

Figure 3   The impossible triangle of the fast fashion industry

Source: myfortytwo

In China, numerous brands that have experienced rapid growth have been built on high investment and low gross margins of the model, offering consumers new styles at a low price. However, without managing the efficiency, they often ultimately find themselves facing inventory issues.

By contrast, SHEIN has achieved success through the management of its supply chain, a strategic approach it has developed over the last decade. Having found a way to address the efficiency, SHEIN has attained profitability whilst maintaining an extraordinary degree of adaptability.

Dressed to the nines: external factors and good timing

Business success is not just about doing the right thing, but also about doing the right thing at the right time. Looking back at the development of cross-border e-commerce and SHEIN's journey, it is apparent that various factors beyond the company's control — China's national policies and global trade policies, the macroeconomic environment, and even the U.S. government's policies — have all to some degree contributed to SHEIN's growth.

For example, in 2016, U.S. President Barack Obama signed a bill to raise the tax exemption limit on imported goods for individuals from USD 200 to USD 800, providing a launchpad for China's export-oriented cross-border e-commerce.

Then in 2018, the trade relationship between the world's two largest economies, China and the United States, started to deteriorate. In response to a new round of tariffs by the U.S., China comprehensively increased its policy support for export-oriented enterprises, to the point where export tax for direct-to-consumer companies was effectively eliminated.

The developing trade war between China and the U.S. mainly impacted B2B companies. SHEIN, with its focus on B2C low-value goods, actually gained a significant tax advantage. With a typical cotton T-shirt being exempt from both the 16.5% import tariff and the 7.5% tax in China, SHEIN enjoyed a price advantage of 24%.

However, it is not clear for how long SHEIN will be able to reap these types of benefits. The U.S. textile industry is, at the time of writing, actively lobbying President Biden to lower the USD 800 duty free import threshold. SHEIN faces risks in some regions due to cultural differences and geopolitical factors, particularly regarding the designs, patterns, and materials of some of its products.

To conclude, SHEIN's success can be attributed to a combination of deliberate strategic choices and fortuitous timing. The long-term vision of SHEIN backed by the tenacity of its management and a strong financial foundation has allowed it to take advantage of opportunities that have arisen, where others might have failed.

While currently facing challenges, such as a hostile global trade policy environment, SHEIN continues to enjoy its unique advantages in cross-border e-commerce through the digitalization of its marketing and supply chain management. Based on an approach that maximizes technological progress and market opportunities, SHEIN has become a model for global expansion.

Updates

- It is estimated that SHEIN generated USD 800 million in net profit in 2022 and USD 23 billion in revenue. The company is reportedly targeting USD 59 billion in sales by 2025.

- SHEIN was valued at USD 100 billion in early 2022, although that valuation declined to USD 64 billion in 2023, partly due to increased competition from rivals such as Temu, an offshoot of Pinduoduo. The two companies have recently slapped lawsuits on each other in U.S. courts, alleging unfair corporate competition.

- Nonetheless, SHEIN still remains among the world's most valuable unicorns. Rumors of an IPO have been denied by the company. If it were to go public, SHEIN would be the most valuable Chinese company to launch a listing since ride-hailing giant DiDi Global made its trading debut in 2021, with a valuation of USD 68 billion. Furthermore, SHEIN is reportedly exploring plans to diversify its manufacturing outside of China, setting up hubs in Mexico, Brazil and India.

The Cream of the Crop

Yili's Ambitions to Build a Global Dairy Company

Tao Zhigang, Professor of Strategy and Economics and Associate Dean for Global Programs, Cheung Kong Graduate School of Business

Qiao Yiyuan, Senior Researcher, Case Center, Cheung Kong Graduate School of Business

Over the three decades since it was established, the Inner Mongolia Yili Industrial Group, also known as Yili, has achieved remarkable success in the dairy industry. With a firm foundation in the domestic Chinese market and a strong internationalization strategy, Yili has emerged as one of the top five dairy companies in the world and aims to be among the top three within the next few years.

Yili is headquartered in Inner Mongolia, a northern Chinese province known for its rich grasslands. To date, Yili has mainly focused on offering dairy products, such as milk, milk powder, yogurt, ice creams and cheese, though the company has recently been expanding its portfolio to include a wider range of products, such as non-dairy beverages.

According to its 2021 annual report, Yili's gross revenue reached over RMB 110 billion (USD 17.1 billion). As per Figure 1, data from Rabobank published in August 2022 shows that Yili had been among the world's top five dairy industry players by revenue for three consecutive years. Yili grew its overall sales volume by 32%, the fastest among the top twenty global dairy companies from January 2021 to June 2022.

What has been Yili's approach to internationalization? And what has the company learned that might be useful for other businesses looking to build a global profile?

Figure 1   Top 10 global dairy brands by turnover, 2022

	USD billion
Lactails, France	26.7
Nestlé, Switzerland	21.3
Danone, France	20.9
DFA, the U.S.	19.3
Yili, China	**18.2**
Fonterra, New Zealand	14.8
Mengniu, China	13.7
Friesland Campina, the Netherlands	13.6
Arla Foods, Denmark/Sweden	13.3
Saputo, Canada	12

Source: Rabobank

The cattle market: from domestic to international

Yili has a long history dating back to 1956, when its predecessor was first established as a dairy cooperative in Hohhot, the capital city of China's Inner Mongolia province. Having undergone various transformations, the Yili Group was founded in 1993 and, in 1996, was listed on the Shanghai Stock Exchange, raising RMB 96.9 million (USD 11.7 million). The company has gone on to achieve massive growth since then.

In the 1990s, the Chinese dairy market faced systemic challenges. At that time, milk production was small-scale and came from numerous producers. Due to the short shelf life of dairy products and supply chain constraints, dairy companies chose to be situated nearby major cities in order to minimize the time in transit and to be located as close as possible to consumers. This made it difficult for them to take advantage of the large-scale production capacity of pastoral areas.

Yili was the first company to introduce ultra-high temperature (UHT) pasteurization to the Chinese market, thereby extending the shelf life of its dairy products by up to eight months and helping address problems associated with choices of business location. The breakthrough allowed the company to develop a large-scale production site in Inner Mongolia, enabling it to serve a much wider market that included developed cities such as Beijing and Shanghai. Yili established contractual relationships with local dairy farmers, ensuring a steady supply of raw milk.

Yili also made full use of financial support from the capital market and the government, which it used to invest in highly automated production facilities. By 2000, the Yili factory in Hohhot was the largest UHT milk production base in China. The company subsequently gained an insurmountable advantage over its competitors, establishing a production and sales network across the country and acquiring significant market share.

To stay ahead of its domestic competitors, Yili invested heavily in R&D to enhance the formulation and processing of dairy products, so as to address the problem of widespread lactose intolerance among Chinese consumers. This helped significantly expand consumer acceptance of dairy products, further boosting product sales. The work of its R&D team enabled Yili to continually expand its product range, extending into new lines such as infant milk powder and organic milk.

In the 1990s when China was less prosperous, Chinese people rarely consumed dairy products. In fact, milk and milk powder were only perceived as nutritious for certain market segments, such as young children, the elderly and the sick. To change people's perceptions, Yili leveraged advertising to build a strong brand. Through a multi-platform advertising campaign, Yili managed to successfully convey the nutritional benefits of milk, positioning itself as a champion of high-quality dairy products.

Thanks to these efforts, by 2003, Yili had become China's foremost dairy company. By 2005, its revenue exceeded RMB 10 billion (USD 1.2 billion). The company's success continued through the decade, boosted by its sponsorship of the 2008 Beijing Olympic Games and the Expo 2010 Shanghai.

However, there were challenges along the way. In 2008, a national scandal erupted when the milk producer Sanlu Group became embroiled in a product safety crisis, which subsequently affected the entire domestic dairy industry. Coinciding with the global financial crisis, Yili, like many other companies, was forced to re-evaluate its strategic plans. After a decade of rapid domestic market expansion, it saw an opportunity to expand outwards and to develop its brand globally, integrating the world's best resources, technology and talent into its processes. The year 2010 marked a turning point for Yili. It rebranded itself, launched a new brand logo and set about taking the first steps as part of its new vision to become a world-class health food group.

In an interview with Harvard Business School, the Yili Chairman and President Pan Gang indicated that the company was aiming to become the world's most trustworthy health food provider. He explained that Yili was pursuing a global ecosystem strategy with the goal of bringing together the world's best dairy resources. Under this strategy, the company established the world's largest integrated dairy production base in New Zealand, undertook joint research initiatives with U.S.-based universities and food-focused R&D centers in Europe and reached vast consumer markets in Asia, Europe, Oceania and the Americas.

The Yili approach to internationalization has focused on three strategic areas: raw materials, technology and markets.

Grass roots: Yili's approach to internationalization

Raw materials

Most of the world's best grazing areas, and therefore primary dairy production regions, are located between the latitudes of 40°-50°, both north and south of the equator. These include areas such as the coasts of the Great Lakes in the U.S., central and western Europe, Inner Mongolia and other parts of northeastern China, certain regions of Australia and New Zealand, Hokkaido in Japan and the Pampas in Argentina. These fertile pastoral regions help make the countries in which they are located natural contenders to be the world's leading suppliers of raw milk.

Yili's plans to meet the world's growing demand for dairy products faced the challenge of physical production limitations. To achieve its growth targets and become globally competitive has required it to establish a presence in these natural resource areas.

In its effort to access high-quality raw materials overseas, Yili has cooperated with enterprises such as Fonterra, New Zealand's largest dairy company and Conaprole, Latin America's largest dairy producer, based in Uruguay. It has also established partnerships with producers in the Netherlands and Denmark to produce dairy products using local milk sources.

Over the past decade, the company has made several strategic business acquisitions.

- In 2013, Yili acquired 100% of the equity interest in Oceania Dairy in New Zealand. After the acquisition, it invested an additional RMB 3 billion (USD 484.4 million) to establish production facilities for infant milk powder, functional milk protein, UHT milk and whole milk powder and to set up a product testing laboratory in New Zealand.
- In 2019, Yili acquired 100% of the equity interest in Westland Co-Operative Dairy Company, the second largest dairy co-operative in New Zealand. After the acquisition, it launched an upgraded production line, significantly increasing the output of the premium grass-fed butter brand "Westgold."

- From 2021 to 2022, Yili took 59% control of Ausnutria Dairy, an international dairy company founded in 2003 in Changsha in China's Hunan province. Ausnutria has a similar strategy to Yili, looking to build overseas raw material production and processing capacity, including through various Dutch dairy acquisition channels, such as Sanimel, Farmel and HGM.

Through these various cooperative agreements and acquisitions, Yili now has 81 global production bases and collaborates with over 2,000 partner companies around the world. Milk supply across the Yili home territory of Inner Mongolia has improved and serves to fill gaps during the off-peak seasons in the northern and southern hemispheres, while mitigating the risk of any unforeseen regional adversities. The strategic synergy in its approach to production has enhanced the company's ability to respond to market demand, to control costs and to guarantee the supply of raw milk.

Technology

From the outset and through its earliest days of domestic expansion, Yili has championed R&D. It has greatly expanded the potential audience for its products in China by improving its formula and providing dairy products suitable for Chinese consumers with lactose intolerance issues. However, on entering the international market, the company found that its competitors, particularly Western-based firms, were already well ahead, having benefited from years of strong economic growth coupled with a long tradition of dairy consumption.

Figure 2 Top 10 dairy exporting countries by volume, and GDP per capita, 2019

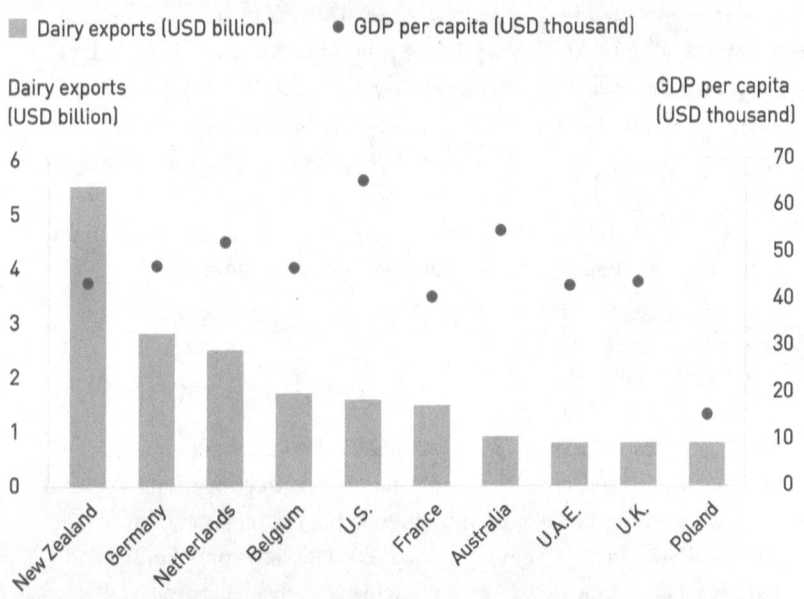

Sources: World Bank, BizVibe, International Trade Centre

Yili recognized that while many mature international markets were highly saturated, rendering them unsuitable targets for entry, there might be opportunities for increasing product competitiveness through high-quality R&D. Therefore, the company undertook research with leading dairy research institutes on projects such as rearing cows for milking, product nutrition, taste and food safety.

In 2014, the company established a European R&D center in the Netherlands focusing on dairy farming, dairy research and food safety, in cooperation with Wageningen University & Research, an institute that is renowned for its expertise in agricultural and forestry sciences. It also signed a cooperation agreement with Lincoln University in New Zealand to establish its Oceania Innovation Center, which focuses on dairy farming and farm management technologies.

During a state visit to the U.S. by Chinese leader Xi Jinping in 2015, Yili took the lead in launching the "SINO-U.S. Food Wisdom Valley" program, bringing together various leading universities in the U.S. and Canada, such as the University of Pennsylvania, Cornell University and the University of Toronto. The Food Wisdom Valley program addresses a broad range of research areas, including nutrition and health, product development, food safety, agricultural science and technology, animal husbandry, veterinary medicine, ecology and environmental protection and business management.

Yili has indicated it has further plans to set up innovation centers in other locations, including in Tokyo, Japan and Bekasi, Indonesia.

Emerging markets

Building on its success in China, Yili has explored growth opportunities in other countries. Rather than entering mature, developed markets and competing with established multinational dairy companies, it has taken the decision to focus on emerging markets with large populations and promising economic development, having already been through this trajectory in the Chinese domestic environment.

Yili initially considered some of the BRICS countries as potential beachheads in which to base its activities. However, the company eventually selected to focus on Southeast Asia, due to its large population base, younger demographic, substantial market development potential, greater cultural similarities and geographic proximity.

Starting in 2015, the company began setting up wholly owned trading subsidiaries in Indonesia, Malaysia, Vietnam and Myanmar to sell its products. It acquired local companies, such as Thai ice cream maker Chomthana, introducing operational efficiencies while learning from the company's cultural expertise and leveraging its domestic reach. In 2020, Chomthana's annual sales in Thailand increased by 68% YoY, providing strong competition to European brands, such as Unilever and Nestlé.

Yili has strategically used investment in emerging markets to expand its reach. In 2019, having had a presence in Indonesia for four years, Yili invested in an ice cream production line in Bekasi. Moreover, some of the international enterprises acquired or invested in by Yili, such as Westland Dairy, Ausnutria Dairy and Chomthana, have themselves gone global, enabling Yili to further expand its international market share.

A cash cow?

Since it first launched its internationalization strategy in 2010, the Yili overseas network has grown and by 2022 comprised 14.8% of the company's total assets, supplying more than 15% of the total raw materials.

In 2018, Yili set up an international business department to focus on developing its presence in overseas markets. From 2018 until 2021, its international revenue grew at a compound annual growth rate of 56%. The first half of 2022 saw a 58% YoY increase in its international business revenue.

In Thailand, Yili's market share in the ice cream sector has risen from 5% to nearly 12%, placing it among the top three players in the market. In Indonesia, the company's market share in the same category has gone from zero to more than 4%, making it one of the top five market players.

Yili's strategy has been based upon the assumption that consumer demand for nutritious foods, particularly dairy products, will develop rapidly due to the growth within local economies. Advancements in dairy farming technology and e-commerce have enhanced the supply capacity of dairy products significantly. At its current rate of expansion, according to Standard & Poor's, even without any further large M&As, Yili could be among the top three dairy companies in the world in sales by 2025, purely based on endogenous growth.

However, domestic factors, such as China's declining birth rate and its aging population, have raised doubts about the prospects for domestic dairy demand. In order to fulfill its stated goal of becoming the world's most trusted health food provider, Yili needs to find new growth opportunities and to increase its presence globally.

Overseas, there have been examples of negative sentiment toward Chinese companies, particularly those working in resource extraction. Complaints have often been based on a perception that Chinese companies are more concerned about acquiring local natural resources than providing employment or supporting the local economy.

With its aforementioned presence throughout Southeast Asia, including its production capacity in Indonesia, businesses in Thailand and sales channels in Vietnam, Myanmar, Malaysia and Singapore, Yili has set out to avoid these types of accusations, by ensuring that the benefits of its operations are shared with local communities. Where possible, it has focused on local procurement and has hired local staff. Building strong economic ties with local entities has also helped Yili enhance the promotion of its products.

More recently, Yili has set its sights on expanding into the African market, which the company believes should have a similar market environment to Southeast Asia.

Peaches and cream: factors behind Yili's success

There are three areas that have been key to Yili's success in internationalizing operations: identifying targets for takeover, localizing overseas operations and choosing the right markets.

Finding realistic M&A targets

Firstly, there is the choice of how to manage a market entry: whether to build from scratch or to acquire an established entity. The latter approach is often preferred, since it tends to provide faster financial results. However, while acquiring larger, more established companies may offer the appeal of faster, higher returns, integrating their management and production structures is often complicated, and may lead to disappointing results.

In order to minimize these kinds of problems, Yili undertakes a stringent evaluation process when considering potential M&A targets. It only acquires businesses that are a good fit with its overall strategy, fill a gap in the Yili ecosystem, offer core competitiveness and promise growth opportunities in its home market, and that are of a size that can be easily absorbed by Yili into its existing ecosystem.

How the integration is managed is also important. While these acquired overseas companies have their own channels and capabilities in their local markets, Yili brings the advanced management capabilities of a top dairy company to further empower them.

Overseas localization

Managing at a distance can be problematic, with overseas operating entities often situated far away from the company's headquarters. Moreover, a management style or technique that works in the home country may not translate well to other markets. Together, these considerations make it even more important to implement appropriate localization strategies in overseas branches.

For Yili, some of the local issues requiring cautious management have included working with the Muslim customs of Indonesia and Malaysia, the Buddhist beliefs of Thailand, the non-English speaking environment and introverted workplace cultures of Japan and the at-times delicate bilateral relationships between Australia, New Zealand and China.

The Yili approach to its overseas operations can be characterized by the Chinese phrase "抓大放小," which translates to "Grasping the large, letting go of the small." At Yili, responsibility for managing financial targets, approving and allocating resources, communicating and implementing high-level strategies and coordinating collaboration among business units falls under the remit of headquarters in China. Day-to-day operations are largely left to overseas entities, which are also provided with a significant degree of autonomy for financial and personnel related decisions.

For example, the New Zealand operating entity retained most of its original personnel after it was acquired by Yili, except for the local resident director and a handful of other employees.

Yili has struck on a successful formula for localization, combining the local team's familiarity with the market and their day-to-day operational experience with HQ's strategic and financial strengths, which together have resulted in positive outcomes.

Choosing a market

Identifying a suitable market for expansion is a two-stage process. The first stage is to choose which specific area of the market to enter. This requires consideration of factors such as the current size and growth rate of an industry, the level of risk in that country — which includes its political stability and openness to foreign investment — the level of competition and maturity within that market and other non-business-related factors such as language, culture and religion.

The second stage is to develop a tailored sales strategy that will align with the specific market's demands. Looking at countries in Southeast Asia, for example, while they may share certain similarities, they each also have unique characteristics that require their own market research, brand positioning and product design considerations prior to entry.

With the emergence of new channels, such as the mobile internet and e-commerce, some of the traditional marketing theories first stipulated in the 1950s, including STP (Segmentation, Targeting, Positioning) and 4P (Product, Price, Place, Promotion), may no longer be fully applicable in vanguard regions of economic development, such as China and the U.S. However, in Southeast Asia, where markets may not yet have fully matured, these theories may still serve as useful guidance and can be used to analyze and evaluate these territories.

Dairy dreaming: Yili's international future

The Yili approach to internationalization has taken a long-term approach in order to deliver tangible, positive results, based on corporate-level strategies, practical and localized tactics and effective execution.

Yili's bespoke approach is reflected in its path to internationalization. In market selection, Yili has initially focused on Southeast Asia, in part due to its similarity to the market in China. In its market entries, the company has considered factors such as the degree of local economic development, infrastructure and the state of bilateral relations with China. The process of analysis has eventually led Yili to, among others, conduct trade in Vietnam, execute M&As in Thailand and build capacity in Indonesia. In choosing the brands for each market, it has carefully considered the maturity of each country and the level of consumer acceptance. In product design, it has taken into account the preferences of local consumers.

To succeed across borders, businesses cannot rely entirely on their previous domestic glories nor stick to the same set of strategies. It is essential to develop different tactics based on the specific circumstances of each market. So far, Yili has shown itself to be highly adept at doing just this.

Updates

- In 2022, Yili's international businesses increased sales by 52% compared to the previous year.
- Yili's total revenue in Q1 2023 reached RMB 33.4 billion (USD 4.7 billion), the strongest single-quarter performance in its history.

Chapter Four

Western Brands Finding Success in China

Many Western brands have managed to carve out their own niche and generate significant success in China's market. By skillfully adapting their products, messaging and consumer engagement strategies to local preferences, brands such as Oatly and KFC have seamlessly embedded themselves in the Chinese consumer's way of life. These success stories provide invaluable lessons on how to thrive in the China market.

Case Studies

9 Milking It for All It's Worth
Oatly's China Market Entry Strategy

10 Fast Food, Fast Success
KFC's Digitalization Strategy in China

Milking It for All It's Worth
Oatly's China Market Entry Strategy

Teng Bingsheng, Professor of Strategic Management and Associate Dean for Strategic Research, Cheung Kong Graduate School of Business

Wang Xiaolong, Senior Researcher, Case Center, Cheung Kong Graduate School of Business

"It's like milk, but made for humans!" is just one of the many humorous campaigns by Oatly, a Swedish oat drink company that entered the Chinese market in 2017. Oatly's flagship product, oat milk, uses a unique enzymatic technology that results in a chemical change when the oats are liquidized. Oatly's oat-based products are now prominently featured in major coffee chains, retail channels and high-end hotels across China. However, while the company's success in the China market came quickly, it did not come easily.

Prior to its China entry, Oatly's key markets had been Europe and the U.S. When he took on the role of President of Greater China, David Zhang (Zhang Chun) had grand ambitions for Oatly in China, aiming to position the brand as the frontrunner in the milk alternatives market in China.

But for Oatly, differentiating itself in a market already crowded with dairy alternatives was a challenge. For thousands of years, the Chinese have consumed non-dairy products, such as soy milk. Purely being a substitute for dairy milk offered less of a potential as a point of difference in China than had been the case in the West.

The company also faced problems in product positioning since it did not fit easily into any pre-existing product category in offline and online shops. In order to address these challenges, Zhang has taken a series of smart, strategic decisions that have contributed to Oatly achieving success well beyond expectations.

Wow! No cow!

The Oatly brand was founded in 2001 by Rickard Öste, a researcher who developed a pioneering enzyme technology that breaks down cereals into a liquid while retaining the main nutrients, providing a dairy-flavored, plant-based drink suitable for lactose-intolerant people. Around the world, the proportion of lactose-intolerant people varies by ethnicity. Oatly decided to initially focus on the lactose-intolerant segment in its marketing and by 2012 the company's revenues had reached USD 29 million a year. At this time, Oatly had not yet extended beyond the Scandinavian market and the company was still a long way from being a world-renowned brand.

In 2012, Oatly appointed Toni Petersson as CEO. With extensive entrepreneurial experience spanning a wide range of sectors, Petersson's approach was markedly different from the previous leadership, with many of the original board members coming from academic backgrounds. Petersson launched a radical organizational change, aiming to incorporate more creativity into the company's DNA. Oatly started to differentiate its brand, taking on the position of a humorous and sustainably-minded "milk challenger," and using slogans such as "Wow! No cow!" To this day, the company continues to disrupt the dairy milk industry, positioning itself as the pioneer of a new generation of protein drinks.

Figure 1 Oatly packaging

Source: Oatly

Oatly's brand vision comprises two key elements: first, helping consumers achieve balance in terms of nutrition and mind; and second, contributing to a more balanced planet. Oatly's main Swedish production plant uses 100% renewable energy and any production materials that are left over are re-used. The company has started using electric trucks to transport its goods in Europe and has integrated sustainable initiatives into the company's annual planning to offset its carbon footprint.

Moving fast into consumer goods

Zhang was the company's first ever employee in Asia and has been instrumental in its success in the region. Prior to joining Oatly, Zhang had spent the previous 20 years working for large companies such as GE, Siemens and other Fortune 500 firms. Zhang has noted, "I had more than 20 years of experience, mainly in the B2B sector, engaging in large-scale equipment sales, industrial projects and engineering contracts with other businesses. I learned that as long as you can convince the decision-makers, you'll get the business. I had very little experience in FMCG (fast-moving consumer goods) but wanted to give it a go. It was a challenging proposition, but the space for entrepreneurship and growth was attractive."

Consumer goods, however, differ significantly from industrial goods. There are low barriers to entry and every consumer is a decision maker. In a large industrial business like GE, there is a consensus that each division of the business should be managed by someone who can adapt to working across various functions and who can lead the team to success. By contrast, the B2C market does not have the same requirements for specific experience within an industry. Rather, success lies in understanding the market, adopting the right strategy and assembling the right team and capabilities. While recognizing the distinct approaches, Zhang also saw similarities in the underlying logic required, and this is what drew him to move over to Oatly and the FMCG sector.

A coffee break into the market

The very first challenge faced by Zhang was how to successfully enter the China market. In the West, Oatly has been launched through retail outlets, which remains the company's primary distribution channel. For various reasons, though, China required a different approach.

In Asia, it is estimated that around 70% – 80% of people have some level of lactose intolerance, with one well-cited study claiming that up to 92% of Chinese individuals are lactose-intolerant.

Chinese consumers are no strangers to plant-based foods, with records of soy milk and tofu being consumed during the Han Dynasty, nearly two thousand years ago. However, this familiarity with the plant-based product category was one of the very first barriers that Oatly faced. Consumers' natural response in China was to consider oat milk as a variation of soy milk, a product which is widely available at low prices. Initially positioning the higher-priced Oatly next to soy milk brands on supermarket shelves proved to be a recipe for failure. At Olé, a supermarket chain, even with the support of in-store promotions, sales were lucky to exceed two or three cartons a day.

After the initial sales flop, Zhang realized he would need a different approach. At that time, in 2018, coffee culture was quickly expanding in China's major cities. Zhang's team saw an opportunity to capitalize on this trend with Oatly's top-selling product, the Barista oat drink, since the company's brand values aligned perfectly with those of coffee-drinking consumers: sustainability-minded, seeking dairy alternatives and within the right price range.

Oatly company representatives individually approached cafés throughout Shanghai, looking for opportunities for product placement and brand exposure. At the heart of this approach was Oatly's "Three Ones" strategy: one city (Shanghai), one market (boutique cafés) and one product (Barista).

While it was initially hard work to convince cafés to try out the product, the quality of Oatly's milk eventually worked to the advantage of the brand, with professional baristas finding that Oatly Barista outperformed alternative products in the preparation of coffee. They recognized that the taste and texture of oat milk were preferred by many consumers over almond or soy milk. With time and persistence, more and more cafés around Shanghai started to use Oatly products in their beverages.

The Barista product is slightly more expensive than many of the alternatives. Zhang smartly used that fact to arouse the curiosity of customers. Oatly encouraged participating cafés to display notices at the counter offering the option to replace a conventional milk latte with an oat milk latte, at a small price premium.

In response to their inquiries, café staff were able to inform customers in a low-key, unassuming manner about Oatly's environmental advocacy, the sustainability benefits of replacing dairy with oat milk, the nutritional advantages of oats and other key messages. The market segment frequenting boutique cafés was able to comfortably absorb the slight price increase associated with a beverage that used Oatly rather than other milk drinks.

Within just a few months, the company had partnered with hundreds of cafés. This led to positive word of mouth within the café sector, thanks to the additional revenue and reinforcement of the brand's identity generated in those cafés using Oatly-based drinks. Having been kicked off by a very deliberate campaign, the brand started to take off organically.

As Oatly's sustainable and health-conscious image became more widely recognized, cafés using its products benefited from the association with these brand values. Those that did not were finding it increasingly challenging to remain competitive. Within a year of launching, by the end of 2018, the company had partnered with more than one thousand cafés, many of them high-end and many of them prominently using Oatly products.

In Europe and the U.S., Oatly had been pitted against the milk industry as a "milk challenger." In China, Zhang actually positioned Oatly alongside dairy in order to cater to consumers' positive perceptions of milk. Using the café channel as a launchpad had helped Oatly to rid itself of the image of being merely a "foreign soy milk." However, in the retail environment, it was still unclear which product category Oatly truly belonged to, leaving Oatly unsure about where to place its products in supermarkets or on online e-commerce platforms, such as Tmall.

The Oatly China team's solution was to develop a new product category, "plant protein" and it was suggested to Tmall that this was how it should be positioned. During the 2018 annual "Singles' Day" shopping festival on November 11, Tmall ran a promotion for this newly-added category. Oatly sold out its stock of 5,000 cartons in 11 minutes flat.

However, the magnitude of demand had not been anticipated, meaning that Oatly Asia was constantly faced with supply shortages. Online sales channels were activated only when there was sufficient stock available. Oatly's manufacturing facilities were overseas, shipping was expensive and there were long lead times of two to three months. As a result, the company was unable to fully meet the demands of the exploding demand in the Chinese market, and with the rise of imitator brands and nonexclusive café partnerships, it was struggling to establish a solid foothold.

Partnering for success

Oatly's success in boutique cafés soon drew the attention of some of the well-known coffee shop chains in China, prompting them to test Oatly products in their stores. By February 2019, Oatly was facing a decision about which of these chains they should partner with in the Chinese market. Negotiations started with Starbucks, the leading chain in China, but faltered due to the conditions demanded by Starbucks and concerns about the reliability of supply.

During the talks, Zhang stressed to his head office how important such a partnership would be in opening up the China market for Oatly. Zhang had three key objectives: he needed a stable supply of products; he wanted increased brand exposure; and he had to find a way to ensure that Oatly was not subjected to any kind of exclusivity agreement. While fending off advances from other coffee chains in China, Zhang believed that the best course for Oatly was to establish its first formal partnership with Starbucks, given the chain's dominant position in China.

For various reasons, negotiations with Starbucks in mainland China stalled. Zhang shifted his focus to the chain's operations in Hong Kong, quickly reaching an agreement with Starbucks there. With Oatly's products available in Starbucks branches in Hong Kong, he went on to sign further agreements with the chain's outlets in Thailand, Singapore, Malaysia and Indonesia.

Increasing sales in these regions led the Starbucks mainland China team to recognize the potential benefits of partnering with Oatly. Eventually, in April 2020, they agreed to sign an agreement to add Oatly oat milk to their beverage options.

By 2022, Oatly's total global revenues reached USD 722.3 million, of which Asia contributed USD 152.8 million, with China making up 88% of that (USD 134 million).

Figure 2 Oatly's global revenue

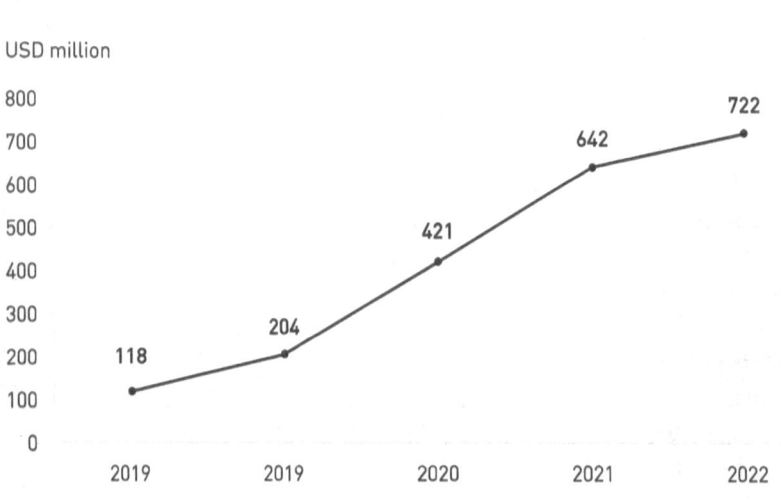

Source: Oatly annual report

Following on from the initial deal, Oatly went on to partner with numerous other outlets.

In China, in addition to Starbucks, Oatly products can also be found in KFC, McDonald's, Pizza Hut, Pacific Coffee and other large chain brands across the food and beverage sector. The heightened recognition resulting from exposure through these prominent brands has helped raise Oatly's profile in retail channels, including supermarkets and convenience stores. With the growth of the Oatly brand in China, the company set up production facilities in Asia, with two factories in eastern China and one in Singapore.

Keeping it fresh

More recently, Oatly has faced the challenge of how to sustain the company's first-mover advantages and branding successes. Over the years, Oatly's success has inevitably given rise to the emergence of numerous imitation brands, including other plant-based and oat drink brands. UBS analysts expect the global plant-based protein market to experience exponential growth, increasing in value from USD 4.6 billion in 2018 to USD 85 billion in 2030.

With oat-based products now generating significant revenue, major brands such as Coca-Cola, Nestlé and Unilever are looking to develop oat milk products, as are international plant-based brands such as Califia and Minor Figure.

Meanwhile, in China, domestic brands including OAKIDOKI, Cereal Planet, OATOAT and Daily Box have emerged. Beverage empires such as Yili and Nongfu Spring have also recently launched new plant-based products in various forms.

Figure 3   Oatly's revenue structure by region

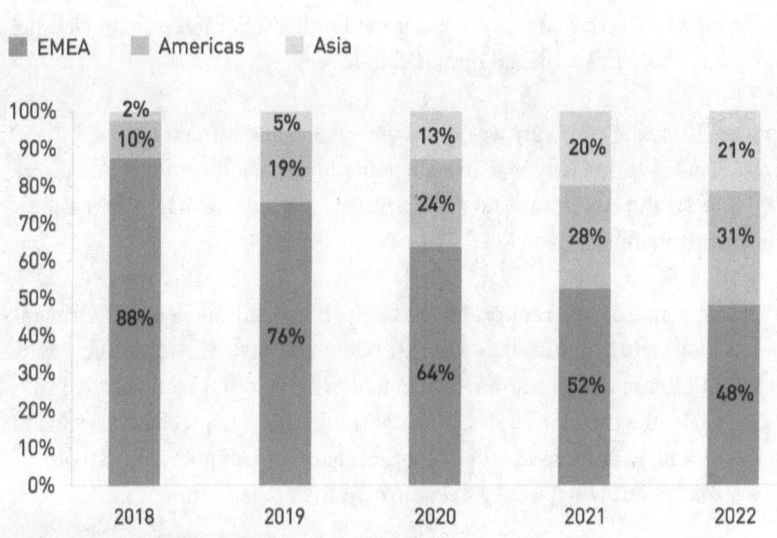

Source: Oatly annual report

Oatly itself has expanded its plant-based brand repertoire, partnering with other manufacturers and launching products such as oat ice cream and oat bakery and pastry products. The company is engaged in other activities to generate business and boost its brand image, such as providing barista training for young people with hearing impairments and promoting Oatly's sustainable recycling programs.

As part of its promotional strategy, Oatly continues to join forces with other brands, most notably Tmall. In December 2020, the first "Tmall Plant Protein Alliance Summit" took place, initiated by Oatly and hosted by Tmall's parent company Alibaba Group, with the aim of discussing "more possibilities for the future of plant-based food."

Planting for the future

Based on a strong foundation of its three-decade long focus on oats and thanks to an effective strategy to enter the food and beverage chain channel in China, Oatly has achieved remarkable success.

In May 2021, the company was listed on Nasdaq and attracted solid investment. While Oatly may have benefited from its first-mover advantage, will it be strong enough to stave off fierce competition which is increasingly coming from all directions?

The emergence of different brands has helped expand the demand for plant-based foods and establish it as a new product category. However, there is a risk that intense competition will lead to a price war that could erode profit margins. While the market in China continues to grow spectacularly, Oatly's status as a high-end brand and its market share are not guaranteed, with many other brands striving to capitalize on the demand for oat milk.

To maintain its China and global foothold, in a colossal global dairy market that has surpassed USD 1 trillion in value, Oatly needs to maximize further opportunities for growth. In addition to its Barista range of coffee-friendly oat milk, the company can leverage its wide range of products and maintain its brand awareness through strong marketing campaigns.

The success of Oatly in China has entailed not just the establishment of a brand but also the creation of an entirely new product category. While it is undeniably facing tough competition, Oatly is well-positioned to continue to enjoy success in the China market, given China's latest carbon neutrality targets, a consumer class that is becoming increasingly brand-conscious, and a growing recognition of the need to do "business for good."

Updates

- Oatly has recently had a bumpier ride. Following on from a 2021 stock market debut that saw the company valued at USD 13 billion, continuing supply issues have dogged the company and dragged down its share price.

- An expected post-COVID-19 tailwind in China has not materialized.

- The company has announced that it will be reducing the range of products it sells and will be refocusing on its core business, namely foodservice and on a small number of retail partners in key cities.

Fast Food, Fast Success
KFC's Digitalization Strategy in China

Sun Baohong, Dean's Distinguished Chair Professor of Marketing, Cheung Kong Graduate School of Business

Huang Xi, MBA Alumnus, Cheung Kong Graduate School of Business

Yan Min, Researcher, Case Center, Cheung Kong Graduate School of Business

In 1987, KFC, one of Yum!'s main brands, opened its first store in China in central Beijing's Qianmen area. KFC's phenomenal growth in China since that time has mirrored that of the economy as a whole. Within ten years, by 1997, KFC had taken a sizeable share of the China market and built a loyal customer base, who saw it as a premium U.S. brand.

After joining the company in 1989, by the mid-1990s, Samuel Su had taken on responsibility for Yum!'s business in Asia Pacific. He recognized the opportunity for China to be the largest market for Yum!. However, knowing that Chinese diners were unlikely to adapt to a purely American menu, Su believed there needed to be a local strategy, rather than one designed by people based at the U.S. headquarters, who were less familiar with the specific environment in China.

Su persuaded Yum!'s senior management to allow him to manage the Chinese business with a degree of operational autonomy. This turned out to be a wise move: by 2015, the China market accounted for more than

50% of Yum!'s total revenue.

Seeking higher returns, shareholders pushed for the Chinese business to be spun off and re-listed as a standalone entity. As a result, Yum China was separated from its parent company.

In 2022, the Yum China operations brought in a revenue of USD 9.6 billion, way higher than Yum!'s revenue from the rest of the world (USD 6.8 billion). KFC has played a major role in this success in China, contributing USD 7.2 billion, accounting for 75% of Yum China's revenue in 2022. By the end of 2022, Yum China had around 13,000 restaurants across China under seven different brands, including KFC and Pizza Hut. KFC had 9,094 stores in China, way more than its competitor McDonald's, which had just 4,978.

Table 1   Yum China's main brands and revenue structure

Million USD

	KFC	Pizza Hut	Others	Total revenue
2020	5,821	1,730	770	8,263
2021	7,003	2,109	993	9,853
2022	7,219	1,960	924	9,569

Source: Yum China annual reports
Note: The fourth column shows the consolidated total revenue adjusted for intercompany transactions. Hence, the sum of the first three columns is different from the value in the fourth column.

KFC's three stages of development

It is possible to identify three key stages of the development of KFC in China to date.

In the first stage, from its entry in 1987 up until around 2000, KFC built the business on the core proposition of it being an American fast-food brand. The classic combination of fried chicken and fries, washed down with a Coke, embodied the very essence of American fast food. It offered a compelling proposition to a Chinese audience that at that time was enjoying the benefits of opening-up and was curious to explore the outside world. The KFC brand was perceived as premium, allowing for a relatively high price point.

From 2000 onwards, KFC began to adjust its offerings, introducing products that appealed to more traditional Chinese tastes, such as its old Beijing chicken rolls — using Peking duck-style hoisin sauce — deep-fried dough sticks — a classic choice for breakfast in China, similar to churros — and other Chinese-style fast food. Behind the scenes, KFC was working to localize its supply chain, including cultivating local suppliers and building its own logistics system. With first- and second-tier cities reaching saturation, KFC began to expand to third- and fourth-tier cities, and the brand started to shift from a high-end to a more affordable positioning and price point.

A third stage of development kicked in around 2013/2014, when KFC found itself facing some of the challenges typical of mature brands. KFC's original customers were getting older and their enthusiasm for the brand had waned over time. For a new generation of consumers, KFC offered nothing new or unusual, particularly when compared with the swathe of new fast-food brands that was emerging and providing increasingly fierce competition. Costs were rising, most notably in first- and second-tier cities and the industry was facing various food safety incidents that impacted demand. Together, these factors contributed to declining profits for the company, forcing a strategic rethink about the future direction of the business.

Hatching a plan

Su and KFC China's management team identified two key ways in which they could transform the business. First, they recognized the need to consolidate KFC's core strengths and optimize its stores, products, services and communications. They understood that these changes could support the second element in KFC's transformation, that is, using digital transformation to empower the KFC business.

In order to consolidate its core strengths, KFC took the decision to concentrate on the values of youth and individuality, adopting a development strategy that encouraged people to "Eat, drink and play, all in one place." It set out to create a warm, casual and stylish atmosphere through its restaurant designs, making them suitable not only for Western-style fast food, but also for other offerings, such as afternoon tea.

Product-wise, the company stuck to its core positioning to "Do chicken right," while at the same time developing more localized products and consistently updating its menu. To improve service and communication, KFC tracked the interests of younger people online, creating new channels to interact with these potential customers, and making full use of partnership opportunities with games, sports, entertainment, culture and other industries. For example, KFC cooperated with TiMi Studios, a subsidiary of Tencent Games, on the popular mobile game "Arena of Valor" to create a themed restaurant, and undertook cross-branding with popular IPs, such as Pokémon.

As for the second strand, digital transformation, KFC set up an internal system review board to research new technologies, to lead the company in upgrading its network infrastructure and to develop and introduce new software. Identifying the growing importance of social media as a channel for communication, the Yum China marketing team took measures to improve their digital marketing skills.

As part of its digital transformation, KFC set out to integrate technology across the customer decision journey and enhance the brand experience. It created a vast membership database to analyze the traffic in its private domain, including its website, social media accounts and stores. In-depth research was conducted to understand customer behavior through the entire customer journey, including pre- and post-meal, to identify pain points and to come up with possible digital solutions through innovation.

Table 2   The KFC dining experience

	Pain points	Solutions
Before arrival	Locating the closest restaurant	• Recommends restaurants based on proximity • Collaborates with Baidu Maps for easier navigation • Recommends special offers
	Queuing	• Permits online ordering and pick up on arrival
In the restaurant	Indecision when ordering	• Adds category navigation and enticing pictures of food to the menu
	Prices and discounts	• Allows customers to save their preferences to "My Menu" • Highlights promotions and combo deals prominently • Adds reward points and coupons to customers' accounts
	Impatience about slow service	• Provides various ways to speed up ordering (ordering screen, mini-app) and payment (WeChat Pay and Alipay)
	Old-style dining decoration	• Introduces themed restaurants, for example with AR games or K-pop experience
After the meal	Dissatisfaction with the experience	• Actively solicits and addresses customer feedback and complaints

Source: CKGSB Case Center

Table 3 The KFC takeout experience

	Pain points	Solutions
Ordering	Customer indecision when ordering/prices and discounts	Similar to dining in solutions
	Large orders for multiple customer groups	Offers group purchases and deals on office orders
Delivery	Delays in delivery	Assigns orders to the closest store to ensure 95% on-time delivery
	Concerns about privacy or infection during the pandemic	Promotes contactless delivery
After-sale service	Customer dissatisfaction with the meal	Similar to dining in solutions

Source: CKGSB Case Center

Digital decision-making

Figure 1 illustrates the eight modules in the customer's decision-making process. Following KFC's digital transformation, the business now has access to a large volume of data that can be used to develop products and design campaigns to attract consumers. Through its social media accounts, the company executes these campaigns and offers coupons, while its digitalized stores enable customers to place orders using their coupons and share their dining experiences at KFC.

Figure 1   KFC's digital transformation roadmap

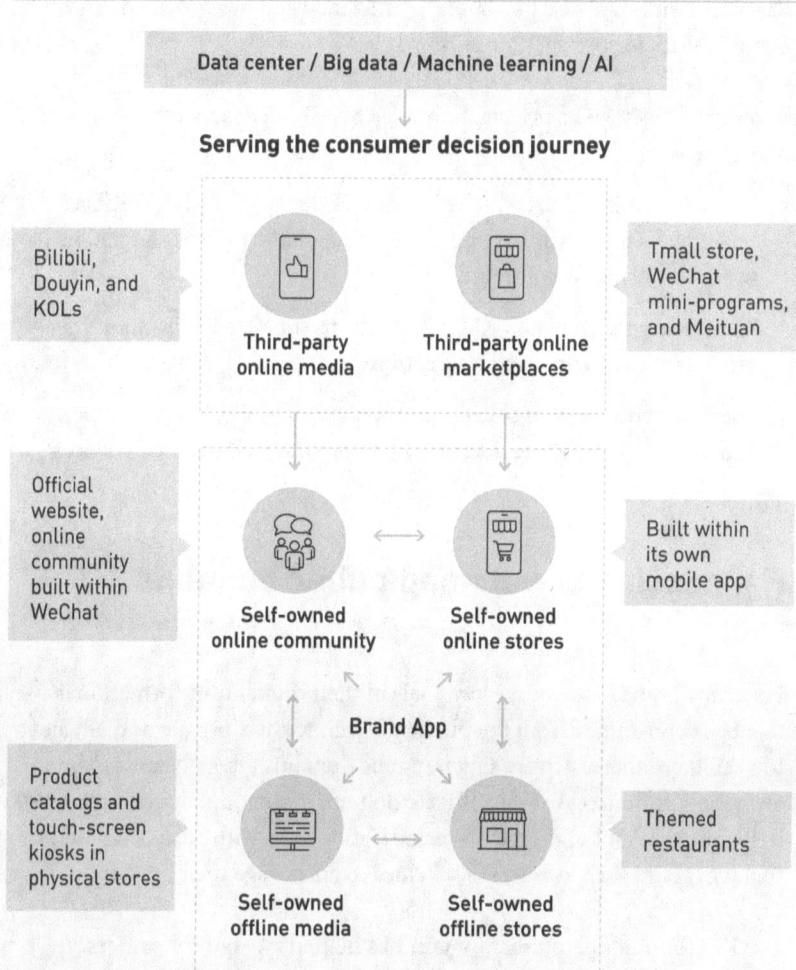

Source: CKGSB Case Center

Among the key contributing elements in KFC's digital transformation have been the building and channeling of traffic to its private domain through the KFC app and other online media and e-commerce platforms, helping drive offline customers to also become online users. In order to better understand customer preferences, a series of AI algorithms has been used to analyze user data, such as their behavior and their product reviews. This has helped improve decision-making efficiency and has provided more opportunities for product innovation.

In order to leverage its private domain, KFC China has focused on three major areas:

- The marketing matrix, which includes KFC's app, website, WeChat account, Weibo (a Chinese microblogging platform) account and its stores on various e-commerce platforms.
- Its mobile app, on which KFC conducts personalized and smart marketing campaigns and interactions.
- The data center, which collects and analyzes users' behaviors, interests and demands, using big data and AI to provide value-added services.

Harnessing private and public domains

For many brands, one of the key goals in their digital transformation is to attract consumers from the public domain to their private domain and to keep them there. Advertising in public domains typically aims to build awareness and increase sales. Private domain marketing, by contrast, tends to be more about building long-term relationships with customers, and can include tactics such as rewards schemes to encourage membership.

For KFC China, the public domain has helped engage consumers through paid advertising, KOLs and social media. The company also has online stores on nearly all of China's third-party marketplaces, including Tmall and Meituan. It continues to utilize traditional offline advertising channels, for example, placing outdoor advertisements on subways, buses and roadways.

On the brand's private domain, KFC has focused on four key self-owned modules: online community, online store, offline media and offline stores.

KFC China runs its online media and e-commerce through channels including its official website, Weibo and through the mini programs on WeChat and Alipay that function similarly to the main app. In addition to its standard stores, KFC also has various music-themed and movie-themed restaurants and futuristic concept stores, as well as various special delivery channels at locations such as gas stations, railway stations and universities.

KFC uses offline catalogs and touchscreen advertisements in offline stores to interact with customers.

Mobile application

Ideally, a mobile application should work to facilitate customer decision-making and purchasing. It should support a brand with digital content and online store options and be able to provide personalized information services to customers at any time, capturing their attention, building customer loyalty and generating conversions.

The functionality and design of the KFC app supports all these objectives. Through the app, KFC encourages customers to get a membership by offering new user benefits and giving away coupons via various channels, including in-store QR codes, WeChat, Alipay and Tmall. When they join, customers immediately receive points and exclusive coupons and accumulate further points with every order they place. Users are able to like and forward things they find on the app to others, which helps maximize user activity and the time spent on the app.

Data center

The notion that users are assets is deeply rooted in the approach of the digital team at Yum China and they have achieved enormous success in building a solid base of online users. By the end of 2022, KFC China had accumulated 380 million registered members, outperforming its domestic competitors, such as McDonald's. It appears to have been more successful than KFC in the U.S. While Yum! does not make its membership figures publicly available, a third-party agency has estimated the active members of the KFC U.S. app at just 10 million, a fraction of the Chinese membership.

The massive user base has provided KFC China with access to a large volume of data and enabled it to build an increasingly accurate understanding of user behavior, which in turn has helped with the delivery of personalized smart marketing services. There are numerous examples of how KFC has made use of data analysis. For instance, intelligent advertising campaigns, coupon distribution and other targeted methods have helped attract customers and have improved their repeat purchase rates. Additionally, purchase value has been raised using coupons that require a certain minimum spending threshold.

Meanwhile, despite having achieved reductions in marketing costs, marketing efficiency has actually increased due to the effective implementation of data analysis. KFC has been able to expand its business scope and develop new sources of profit growth. For example, when customers place an online order, they have the option to purchase a membership card and vouchers for customized offers to be redeemed later.

With this highly advanced digital infrastructure already in place, KFC China is well positioned to undertake further digital transformation during the next era of digitalization, Web3.

Measuring the digital payoff

Cost reduction has been among the key objectives in the KFC China. Sales and marketing expenses for Yum China as a percentage of operating revenue have decreased, from 4.76% in 2014 to 3.78% in 2021. In terms of revenue, Yum China's EBIT and EBITDA have both grown steadily during the transformation process. The company's net profit margin grew from close to zero in 2014 to 10.4% in 2021.

Efficiency has improved, with the fixed asset turnover ratio increasing from 3.6 in 2015 to 4.9 in 2021. Sales per employee have increased from RMB 112,200 (USD 18,010) in 2015 to RMB 139,600 (USD 21,643) in 2021. Net profit per employee has increased even more markedly, from RMB 5,200 (USD 835) in 2015 to RMB 14,000 (USD 2,170) in 2021.

The impact of the COVID-19 pandemic saw revenues and profits decline among many restaurant chains. Yum China appears to have weathered the storm, thanks in large part due to its high level of digitalization. In 2022, 89% of revenue from KFC and Pizza Hut restaurants was generated through digital ordering and KFC China's 380 million community members accounted for around 62% of total sales.

Thanks to its investments in technology and the range of technological innovations it has implemented, KFC is sometimes even referred to as "a technology company that sells fried chicken." This case study has focused on the outward-facing digitalization of KFC, but many other key areas of the company, such as supply chain, logistics and inventory management, have also benefited from advances in digitalization. In 2021, Yum China opened digital R&D centers in Shanghai, Nanjing and Xi'an, utilizing a wide range of technologies to develop new solutions and services to further drive the company's end-to-end digitalization.

For Yum China, digital transformation has been a critical element in enhancing the company's competitiveness. Joey Wat, CEO of Yum China, has explained, "We use digital technology to continually strengthen the company's core competencies and to forge a stronger business model for long-term growth." KFC China's investment in digitalization certainly appears to have paid off.

Table 4   Examples of KFC's sales strategies in different countries and regions

	United States	China	Europe	Southeast Asia
Products	Continues to focus on fried chicken, burgers and french fries.	Focused on localization and innovation, with launches such as "Old Beijing" chicken rolls, breakfast porridge, and fried dough sticks.	Focused on localization and innovation, with launches such as British veggie burgers and Italian lasagna.	Focused on localization and innovation, with launches such as Thai fried rice and Indian curry chicken.
Promotion	Advertized via a range of media; attracted customers with gifts, free samples and fun packaging.	Promoted through various coupons and discounts, such as Crazy Thursday; cooperated with charities and well-known IPs.	Engaged in various promotional activities, including discounts, coupons, and giveaways. Often partnered with local media, sporting events, and charities.	Focused on interactivity and participation, featuring interactive game promotions and themed campaigns during local festivals.
Market expansion	Supported franchises to expand market coverage and penetration.	Maintained a sharp focus on the construction and management of direct sales restaurants, ensuring a consistent standard of quality and service.	Covered cities, suburbs, airports, railway stations.	Focused on expanding channels by opening in diverse locations, including shopping centers, railway stations, and airports.

	United States	China	Europe	Southeast Asia
Pricing	Standardized strategy according to unified cost and profit calculations, for unified pricing.	Utilized a differentiated pricing strategy, formulating prices based on consumer groups, products, periods, and regions.	Set higher prices in Europe due to elevated local quality and health standards, resulting in greater brand trust.	Kept prices relatively low in Southeast Asian markets due to local consumption levels and competitor pricing.
Brand focus	As a Western-style food brand, KFC emphasized "global consistency," innovation, and competitiveness.	Concentrated on localizing the U.S. brand to the Chinese market while emphasizing initiatives related to social responsibility and public welfare.	Prioritized health, quality, environmental protection, as well as eco-friendly products and packaging.	Embraced creativity and fun, often collaborating with popular IPs to introduce limited edition products and themed restaurants.

Source: CKGSB Case Center

Updates

- Yum China reported a profit plunge of nearly 90% in the fourth quarter of 2022, the result of a widespread COVID outbreak hitting the business.
- The earnings outlook for 2023 is also somewhat bleak, with sales reportedly softening.

Faculty
Biographies

Jing Bing
荆兵

Associate Professor of Marketing,
Cheung Kong Graduate School of Business

PhD, University of Rochester

Jing Bing is Associate Professor of Marketing at CKGSB. He earned his PhD in business administration from the University of Rochester in 2001.

Between 2001 and 2007, he was Assistant Professor of Information Systems at the Stern School of Business at New York University. Professor Jing's research interests include mass customization, product line design and pricing, product differentiation, word-of-mouth marketing, etc.

His work has appeared in leading scholarly journals and he served on the editorial board of *Marketing Science*.

Li Wei
李伟

Professor of Economics, Associate Dean for Asia and Director of the Case Center, Cheung Kong Graduate School of Business

PhD, University of Michigan

Li Wei is Professor of Economics, Associate Dean for Asia and Director of the Case Center at CKGSB. He was formerly a professor (with tenure) at the Darden Graduate School of Business Administration, University of Virginia and he also taught at Duke University's Fuqua School of Business.

An authority on Chinese economy and business, Dr. Li's main research focus is on economic development, taxation, financial markets, corruption, corporate governance, corporate research and development, entrepreneurship, trade and investment in China. His monthly Business Conditions Index (BCI) has been widely followed by the public and featured by prominent media. Professor Li has extensive consulting experience with multinational firms, Chinese firms and the World Bank.

Cheung Kong Graduate School of Business

Song Zhongzhi
宋忠智

Associate Professor of Finance, Shanghai Jiao Tong University

Former Assistant Professor of Finance, Cheung Kong Graduate School of Business

PhD, University of British Columbia

Song Zhongzhi is a former Assistant Professor of Finance at CKGSB. He now serves as Associate Professor of Finance at Shanghai Jiao Tong University.

He focuses on asset pricing, technology and macro-finance and the Chinese capital markets. He has published in influential journals such as *Review of Finance*, *Management Science* and *Journal of Financial Economics*. Professor Song received his PhD from University of British Columbia.

Sun Baohong
孙宝红

Dean's Distinguished Chair Professor of Marketing, Cheung Kong Graduate School of Business

PhD, University of Southern California

Sun Baohong is Dean's Distinguished Chair Professor of Marketing at CKGSB. Previously, she was Carnegie Bosch Professor of Marketing at the Tepper School of Business of Carnegie Mellon University.

Her research focuses on rational and strategic consumer choices and dynamic structural models, dynamic and interactive marketing mix and customer information management, and, most recently, on modeling dynamic and inter-dependent consumer decisions on e-commerce and social media platforms.

Professor Sun is the recipient of numerous awards for research and teaching, and she serves on the editorial boards of *Journal of Marketing Research*, *Marketing Science*, and *Journal of Marketing*. She also has extensive consulting experience with major corporations including Bosch, Boy Scouts of America, Highmark Insurance, John Deer and IBM.

Tao Zhigang
陶志刚

Professor of Strategy and Economics and Associate Dean for Global Programs, Cheung Kong Graduate School of Business

PhD, Princeton University

Tao Zhigang is Professor of Strategy and Economics and Associate Dean for Global Programs at CKGSB. His areas of expertise include economics of strategy and organization, China business and economy, and international economics.

He taught at the University of Hong Kong from 1998 to 2021, and at Hong Kong University of Science and Technology from 1992 to 1998. Professor Tao received his B.Sc. in management science from Fudan University in 1986, and PhD in economics from Princeton University in 1992. He has published in various economics and management journals, and his work has been widely cited.

Teng Bingsheng
滕斌圣

Professor of Strategic Management and Associate Dean for Strategic Research, Cheung Kong Graduate School of Business

PhD, City University of New York

Teng Bingsheng is Professor of Strategic Management and Associate Dean for Strategic Research at CKGSB. He formerly served as a tenured Professor of Strategic Management at George Washington University (GWU), where he was a doctoral advisor and lead professor of the departmental doctoral program.

Professor Teng has widely published in academic journals and his research is included in textbooks on strategic management. An authority on strategic alliances, he is regularly interviewed by international media.

Professor Teng is a member of the *Academy of Management* and serves on the editorial board of *International Entrepreneurship and Management Journal*. He has received many awards for his research, and his biography appears in *Who's Who in America* and *Who's Who in American Higher Education*. He was named as a Highly Cited Chinese Researcher by Elsevier during 2014 and 2020.

Xiang Bing
项兵

Founding Dean and Professor of China Business and Globalization, Cheung Kong Graduate School of Business

PhD, University of Alberta

Xiang Bing is the Founding Dean and Professor of China Business and Globalization at CKGSB.

Professor Xiang is a leading authority on China business, innovations in China, globalization of Chinese companies, China's development models, global implications of China's transformation, social innovation, economic disruptions, China-U.S. relations, global trade and investment systems and global governance. His writings and cases on these subjects are considered among the most influential in China and beyond.

Professor Xiang has served as an independent board member of a number of companies (including four Fortune Global 500 companies) listed in Hong Kong, Mainland China and the United States. He advises many reputable global universities and organizations and has served as a keynote speaker at influential forums and conferences around the world.

Zhu Yang (Leon)
朱阳

Professor of Operations Management,
Cheung Kong Graduate School of Business

PhD, University of Florida

Zhu Yang (Leon) is Professor of Operations Management at CKGSB. Prior to joining CKGSB, Leon was a tenured full professor at the Data Sciences and Operations Department of the Marshall School of Business at University of Southern California. He received his Ph.D. in Industrial and Systems Engineering and M.A. in Economics from the University of Florida, and Bachelor's degree from Shanghai Jiaotong University. Before joining Marshall, he was a Postdoc and lectured at the University of California, Berkeley.

Professor Zhu has been accepted by or published in various academic journals, including the *Academy of Management Review, American Economic Review, Journal of Economic Theory, Management Science, Manufacturing and Service Operations Management, Operations Research, Production and Operations Management,* and *Rand Journal of Economics*. He also serves as Associate Editor or Senior Editor for *Operations Research, Manufacturing and Service Operations Management,* and *Production and Operations Management,* among others.

About CKGSB
Case Center

https://english.ckgsb.edu.cn/worldwide/insights/case-center/

In 2003, just one year after CKGSB was established, it inaugurated its Case Center. The center is dedicated to researching and creating business case studies, showcasing the practices and progress of businesses primarily in China and Asia, but also around the globe.

With a growing library, currently comprising more than 500 cases, the center aims to provide both practical and theoretical insights into management. Each case study is led by a CKGSB professor and is typically based upon exclusive interviews conducted with senior executives from renowned companies. The Case Center is led by Li Wei, a distinguished member of our macroeconomics faculty, who serves as CKGSB's Professor of Economics and Associate Dean for Asia.

The Center's research spans fields including strategy, management, globalization, economics, marketing, operations, finance and accounting. It features companies of diverse sizes and developmental stages, representing a wide spectrum of industries.

Our case studies describe business achievements and investigate the lessons learned by industry leaders. Since the 2019 publication of our inaugural case studies book, *China in Transition*, the center has expanded its focus to encompass several emerging issues reshaping the business landscape, such as digitalization, green transition, social innovation as well as entrepreneurship and unicorns.

By exploring how pioneers are changing and adapting to these major shifts, the Case Center aims to illuminate the strategies that enable a successful business to stay competitive, diversify across sectors and markets, and strategically plan for the future.

CKGSB's cases provide business insights for a wide-ranging audience. Our work has appeared in top-tier global media, such as *The Financial Times*, *Harvard Business Review*, *Caixin* and *Caijing*.

The Case Center has also produced several case books in Chinese. The most recent publication focused on how Chinese companies have employed innovative approaches in their strategies, business models, production and brand tactics to overcome market and technological changes.

About Cheung Kong Graduate School of Business

https://english.ckgsb.edu.cn/

Established in November 2002, Cheung Kong Graduate School of Business (CKGSB) aims to cultivate transformative business leaders with a global vision, social responsibility, innovative mindset, and ability to lead with empathy and compassion.

CKGSB provides cutting-edge insights into the latest developments in Asia and their consequential impact on global business dynamics. Our distinguished faculty comprises over 40 full-time professors, each with extensive experience in Chinese business and a background teaching at prestigious institutions, where more than half received tenure. Notably, three CKGSB professors have held the esteemed role of inaugural Chief Strategy Officers at leading digital giants Alibaba Group, Ant Group and JD.com, while continuing to contribute to the school's teaching and research efforts.

CKGSB offers a range of innovative degree and non-degree programs, including MBA, Executive MBA, Business Scholars Program and Executive Education programs in multiple languages. The school boasts a strong alumni network of over 20,000 executives, with more than half occupying CEO or Chairman positions, and collectively overseeing one-fifth of China's most valuable brands. Moreover, 96% of our Executive MBA students hold key decision-making positions in China's largest private, state-owned, and multinational companies.

CKGSB has carved out a niche in business education since 2015, pioneering specialized programs tailored for unicorn founders and aspiring unicorns in collaboration with prominent companies such as Alibaba, Amazon, Baidu, ByteDance, JD.com, Microsoft (China), SenseTime and Tencent. These programs have guided over 1,000 founders, including those behind 38 unicorn companies listed by CB Insights from 2017–2022. CKGSB has also expanded this initiative overseas, launching the first global series of unicorn programs through partnerships in Dubai, Singapore, Seoul, Milan, Berkeley, New York and Stanford.

CKGSB transcends conventional boundaries of business schools, collaborating with businesses, governments, multilateral institutions, non-profit organizations and civil society to address some of humanity's most pressing issues such as income inequality, social immobility and sustainability. The school has made the humanities a core part of its business curriculum since 2005, ensuring its students possess a holistic understanding of business. To showcase its commitment to societal progress, CKGSB established the EMBA philanthropy scholarship in 2002. Today, this scholarship is awarded across all degree programs to exceptional leaders in civil society and NGOs. Additionally, since 2010, all degree students are mandated to engage in philanthropic service, accumulating over 165,000 hours of service to date. Acknowledging the importance of multi-stakeholder collaboration, CKGSB made 'social innovation' a required module for all degree programs since 2018. In 2021, the school launched a mandatory "Social Innovation and Business for Good" field course for EMBA students, empowering over a thousand executives to incorporate ESG principles into the core of their businesses.

CKGSB is headquartered in Beijing, with additional campuses in Shanghai and Shenzhen, and representative offices in New York, London and Hong Kong.

For more information, please visit: https://english.ckgsb.edu.cn/

www.ingramcontent.com/pod-product-compliance
Lightning Source LLC
LaVergne TN
LVHW030343070526
838199LV00067B/6432